CLOSE TO THE EDGE

WITHDRAWN
UTSA LIBRARIES

CLOSE TO THE EDGE

In Search of the Global Hip Hop Generation

Sujatha Fernandes

VERSO
London • New York

First published by Verso 2011
© Sujatha Fernandes 2011

All rights reserved

The moral rights of the author have been asserted

1 3 5 7 9 10 8 6 4 2

Verso
UK: 6 Meard Street, London W1F 0EG
US: 20 Jay Street, Suite 1010, Brooklyn, NY 11201
www.versobooks.com

Verso is the imprint of New Left Books

ISBN-13: 978-1-84467-741-2

British Library Cataloguing in Publication Data
A catalogue record for this book is available from the British Library

Library of Congress Cataloging-in-Publication Data
A catalog record for this book is available from the Library of Congress

Typeset in Minion Pro by MJ Gavan, Truro, Cornwall
Printed in the US by Maple Vail

Library
University of Texas
at San Antonio

For Mike Walsh

Contents

Preface

Don't push me 'cause I'm close to the edge
I'm trying not to lose my head
It's like a jungle sometimes, it makes me wonder
How I keep from going under.
—Grandmaster Flash and the Furious Five, "The Message"

Late one Friday night in my teenage years, I was watching the Australian music video show *rage*, and I saw a flashback video of the 1982 rap hit "The Message." I was growing up in Maroubra—a working-class beachside neighborhood of Sydney that was bordered by a jail, a sewage treatment plant, and the project-like Coral Sea Housing Commissions. I was captivated by the raw and angry lyrics that laid bare ghetto realities in Reagan's America. Back then I didn't know the story behind the song—that, although it was credited to the legendary Grandmaster Flash and the Furious Five, it was mostly written and recorded by a session musician not even in the band, and the band members who appeared in the video were lip-synching to the song. But there was something fitting about my close identification with a fabricated product that revealed so many truths. Any imagined connection I felt to an American ghetto was contrived at best, yet—and I don't know why—the song struck a chord with me.

My interest in hip hop had begun with lessons in b-boying at a workshop run by the Randwick Municipal Council. After we saw Michael Jackson's video clip *Thriller*, all the kids at my school wanted to do the moonwalk. But, unlike the b-boys and b-girls in the Bronx, who developed the dance styles at house parties, outdoor jams, and school hallways, we were taught the moves by our local city authorities. I was mesmerized by the scratching and raw energy of rapping in Run-DMC's "Walk This Way" on *Countdown*, a music show presented by an Egyptologist in a cowboy hat named Molly.

Salt, Pepa, DJ Spinderella, and Neneh Cherry were my role models and my guide to male-female relationships through the angst of adolescence. They created images of black beauty and sexuality that had not been available to us in Australia. When they talked back to men—"Don't you get fresh with me," and "Yeah, you, come here, gimme a kiss"—they inverted the game of male pursuit that we had come to see as the norm. My friends and I would go to the downtown clubs like Kinselas to dance and hear the latest music. We used the music to escape the small and parochial world of our classmates—of Saturday night drinking binges and casual hookups at local working-class pubs known as Returned Servicemen's Leagues (RSLs).

My growing fascination with rap music paralleled my political awakening. At college in the early 1990s, I joined a youth organization, Resistance, and became a full-time activist. At the time I was spending hours in the secondhand music stores along Pitt Street downtown, discovering records from Boogie Down Productions, Digable Planets, Public Enemy, and A Tribe Called Quest. My cousin Miguel Dsouza had the first hip hop radio show in Sydney, where I heard political rap from the States. The godfathers of rap, The Last Poets, had prophesized that the revolution was coming. It seemed that, with the intifada in Palestine, the Fretilin guerrillas in Indonesia-occupied East Timor, and rebellious youth facing down tanks in the streets of Jakarta and Durban, global revolt was imminent. So why didn't anyone on my block know it?

It finally dawned on me one day. I was with other, mostly white, activists, handing out leaflets at Sydney's town hall to protest the spate of deaths of Aboriginals while in police custody. But all the Aboriginal kids were walking right on past us. Just around the corner b-boys had laid out their cardboard strip and were doing head spins and windmills. I watched the crowd—immigrant, Aboriginal, and white kids—that was gathering around them. I realized then that hip hop culture was speaking to them in a way that we activists were not—could not. It was this revelation that sparked my quest to find a global hip hop generation. Afrika Bambaataa had talked about a "Universal Zulu Nation." KRS-One had rapped, "In every single 'hood in the world I'm called Kris." Chuck D had described the collective consciousness of a black planet. Inspired by these spokespersons for a new era, I began what would become an eleven-year odyssey across four countries in search of what exactly it was that made hip hop such a powerful global force.

But before I take readers on this journey, I want to rewind a little, to think about how hip hop went global in the first place.

The Making of a Hip Hop Globe

Pedro Alberto Martínez Conde, otherwise known as Perucho Conde, was probably the first rapper to compose a hit song outside the United States. A poet and comedian from the inner-city Caracas barrio of San Agustín, Conde was perplexed by the strange but catchy lyrics of the Sugar Hill Gang's 1979 hit "Rapper's Delight." In 1980 he came up with a Spanish version that went to the top of the charts in Latin America and Spain.

Far from the outdoor jams and battles of the Bronx scene where hip hop originated, "Rapper's Delight" was packaged and designed for travel. But that didn't mean global audiences got it. Conde baptized his imitation "La Cotorra," the term for a pompous and long-winded speech. Other take-offs surfaced from Jamaica to Brazil; in Germany the song was called "Rapper's Deutsch." Cubans called it "Apenejé," because nobody could make sense of the lyrics. As the first rap song to go global, "Rapper's Delight" embodied the mix of fascination and incomprehension that would accompany the spread of early rap.

By the early 1980s the global circulation of hip hop through the music industry was being paralleled by the efforts of hip hop ambassadors like Afrika Bambaataa to spread a message of black brotherhood and unity. Back in 1973 Bambaataa had founded the Universal Zulu Nation, a Bronx-based street organization that drew on the mythology of anticolonial South African warriors to redirect the energies of inner-city gang youth. In April 1982 Bambaataa released his single "Planet Rock," an anthem for this nascent movement, which was producing chapters across the city. With its mix of European technorock, funk, and rapping, "Planet Rock" was a model of fusion that imagined unity across cultures the same way Bambaataa had created unity across gang lines.

As he toured Europe and England in November, Bambaataa hoped to set the groundwork for the global spread of his movement. North African immigrant youth in the *banlieues*, or suburban peripheries, of Paris were attracted to Bambaataa and his message of black solidarity. Local chapters sprung up in Britain and Japan, where Bambaataa toured in 1985. In Brazil adherents like King Nino Brown preached "knowledge of self" and experience as the foundations of hip hop.[1] Bambaataa imparted an Afrocentric and socially conscious ethos to his global hip hop followers.

Bambaataa's mission, to forge a global hip hop community, echoed the aspirations of the Pan-Africanist Marcus Garvey. His mission was taken up by the next three generations. Chuck D of Public Enemy took Garvey's vision of a black planet around the globe in the late 1980s, visiting local communities while on foreign tours. The Black August Hip Hop Project was formed in the late 1990s to draw connections between radical black activism and hip hop culture. The group organized exchanges between militant rappers in the US, Cuba, and South Africa. And the new millennium was the era of diasporic rappers, who forged a politics of global solidarity from within the heart of empire.

These hip hop ambassadors had their counterparts among intellectuals such as Paul Gilroy, who proposed the concept of the "Black Atlantic" as a space of exchange, belonging, and identity among Afrodiasporic communities that surpassed national boundaries.[2] Music held a privileged place in the Black Atlantic, unseating the primacy of language and writing as expressive forms. But blackness did not always have to be the element connecting marginalized communities. George Lipsitz saw "Planet Rock" as part of an international dialog built on the imagination of the urban poor internationally who were suffering from the effects of global austerity policies imposed by transnational capital.[3] Another set of scholars has more recently used the trope of the Global Hip Hop Nation to express the diffusion of hip hop and its social location as a universal cultural space.[4] All these scholars saw the potential of the market for carrying important political ideas between cultures.

My own quest in this book mirrors the project of these ambassadors and scholars. Could hip hop create a fellowship of marginalized black youth around the globe? Could rappers be the voice not just of a post–civil rights generation in the American ghettos but of a generation of young people in the *cités*, housing projects, barrios, and peripheries of urban metropolises worldwide that has been excluded from the promises of a new global economy? Was there such a thing as a global hip hop generation, and could it act politically?

As I traveled the globe in search of this elusive community, I saw the ways that hip hop was being integrated into the arsenal, repertoire, and landscape of urban youth. Yet the more I probed, the more I became aware of the disconnect between localized expressions of hip hop. If something held them together, it was being lost in a haze of misunderstandings, cultural assumptions, and mixed signals. My own projected imaginings and desires were not being met with the enthusiasm I expected. The easy alliance of a hip hop globe was in danger of being rejected as a fantasy concocted and imposed by the West and rejected by the rest.

The same year "Planet Rock" was released, the single called "The Message" came out. It was credited to Grandmaster Flash and the Furious Five. Where "Planet Rock" preached universal brotherhood and transcendence, "The Message" was an edgy take on ghetto life. Where Bambaataa envisaged a universal consciousness, "The Message" was concerned with the specifics of everyday survival.[5] Produced by Sugar Hill Records—the same label that released "Rapper's Delight"—"The Message" was another manufactured product. At the same time, "The Message" came to represent a profound counterforce in global hip hop history. And it offered a lesson that could not be ignored.

Exactly this local specificity emerged as key in the global

spread of hip hop. Hip hop was shaping a language that allowed young people to negotiate a political voice for themselves in their societies. As I learned through my travels, the genesis of hip hop in each case was highly dependent on the history, realities, and constrictions hip hoppers faced from within their own context. The Hip Hop Nation as a transnational space of mutual learning and exchange may not have been a concrete reality. But the transient alliances that hip hoppers imagined across boundaries of class, race, and nation gave them the resources and the platform they needed to tell their stories and provided the grounds for their locally based political actions.

Global hip hop was always marked by a tension between the desire for transcendence and the need to speak directly to local realities. As the hip hop journalist Jeff Chang has said, the incongruous visions of "Planet Rock" and "The Message" could be brought together only on the dance floor.[6] The music held spaces of possibility for unity and cross-cultural understanding that made it powerful. Yet the contradictions between the dual visions at the core of the culture would be replayed throughout global hip hop history.

My motivation for writing this book lies in the abyss that I encountered as I came of age in Sydney in the eighties. In the seventies and early eighties I was surrounded by social ferment and political engagement. I now look back on that time as one when people considered radical change a real possibility. I remember my dad and his brothers debating anarchism. During our school vacations my sister and I were sent to stay with my auntie Dina in western Sydney. I witnessed her work in the refuge movement, which protected women from domestic violence. I read about feminism and racism in the books in my auntie Joyce's house—Germaine Greer's *Female Eunuch* and Toni Morrison's *The Bluest Eye*. I began a correspondence with my mum's cousin Nigel, a socialist activist who was working with the Pintubi Aboriginal peoples in the Northern Territory.

I reached adolescence in the mid-1980s. Unemployment was high because of a serious economic recession, public sector cutbacks, and the decline of manufacturing industries, all inspired by Thatcher- and Reagan-style free-market policies. The glass factory and Resch's Waverly Brewery on South Dowling Street were shut down and the old buildings lay abandoned, their windows cracked and blackened. In the working-class beachside neighborhood where I grew up, youth unemployment fueled problems of heroin addiction, crime, and violence between rival surf gangs. On cold winter mornings the beach was lined with idle youth, smoking weed or surfing. And the people around me gradually withdrew from politics and into their private lives.

Hip hop was one way out of the void I found myself in. In the conscious rhymes of KRS or the funky wisdom of Salt-N-Pepa, I found a path to political awareness. And I met others who had also found a voice through hip hop, as they too compared the political vibrancy of their parents' generation—from the Aboriginal land rights movement to the Cuban revolution—with the bleak political landscape in which hip hoppers came of age. In the media and in popular culture, our generation was labeled Generation X—the ignored generation, the nihilist generation, the apolitical generation. But these labels didn't describe the angry and politicized young people I saw embracing hip hop culture. Bakari Kitwana had used the phrase "hip hop generation" to describe African Americans who came of age in the post–civil rights era.[7] Given the conditions of unemployment, incarceration, and poverty afflicting not just African Americans, but young people from the *banlieues* of Paris to the hillside shanties of Rio, I wondered whether we could talk about such a thing as a global hip hop generation.

I traveled to Havana in the late 1990s, where I witnessed the formation and maturation of Cuban hip hop. Havana was the site of an international hip hop festival. I thought that on this revolutionary island I would find the kinds of transnational solidarities that made the Hip Hop Nation powerful. Not only was this global solidarity a mirage, but Cuba didn't seem as revolutionary as I had hoped. It would take a crisis from the North for me to appreciate the strategic ways in which Cuban rappers negotiated both their revolution and their place on the hip hop globe.

Meanwhile, I was living in Chicago and checking out the hip hop scene by night. What struck me was the value that Chicago hip hoppers placed on independence, especially after I'd witnessed Cuban rappers' reliance on the state. Did this multi-ethnic city hold the possibility for building an autonomous and truly diverse Hip Hop Nation? The city's segregation presented serious obstacles. This took me back to my participation in hip hop in Australia during the mid-1990s and forward to Caracas in the new millennium, where hip hop was tied in to networks of grassroots activism. When our generation came together as a political force, we could find fleeting moments of connection. But, as the Paris and Redfern (Sydney) riots would reveal, some of the most powerful uprisings of the hip hop generation came not from international alliances of activists and rap celebrities, but from the everyday struggles of ghetto communities around the globe.

Of course, one of the central issues of the book remains: Who is the "we" that makes up the global hip hop generation? The easiest part of the answer is the age group—Kitwana defines the hip hop generation as those born between 1965 and 1984. So that would include those of us now in our midtwenties to mid-forties. The harder part is the social demographics of that group. Chang tells us that the hip hop generation includes "anyone who is down."[8] But, if we think of the historically marginalized communities where hip hop emerged, and the housing projects and tenements across the globe where it resonated, the global hip hop generation would not include an Australian Indian female with a doctoral degree and the means to travel around the world. In this book I use my personal narrative as a way to reflect on the nature and scope of the global hip hop generation. Underlying all my endeavors is the hope that some universal thread connects all of us who have been brought together through hip hop culture, especially those in the most vulnerable and impoverished sectors. But I also came to the realization that privilege—whether by birth or acquired, of skin color, nationality, or social class—would always inhibit the attempt to create global communities.

The early elements of hip hop culture to travel internationally consisted largely of graffiti and the dance style known as b-boying. The 1982 tour of Afrika Bambaataa and the Soulsonic Force had included the pioneering b-boys of the Rock Steady Crew, the Double Dutch Girls, the DJ Grandmixer DST, and the graffiti writers FUTURA and DONDI. The small audiences that turned up at the venues on the European tour were able to witness these elements of hip hop culture live.[9] For the rest of the world, knowledge of graffiti and b-boying came from television and visual culture.

The classic 1982 film *Wild Style*, produced and directed by Charlie Ahearn, was a tribute to the elements of the culture. It was released in cinemas worldwide, including Japan, where the cast of the film went to promote it. Many global fans had their first glimpse of b-boying in the Hollywood blockbuster *Flashdance*, released in 1983. In one brief scene Rock Steady Crew members b-boy to Jimmy Castor's "It's Just Begun." Over the next few years Hollywood capitalized on the international success of Rock Steady's *Flashdance* cameo. Tinseltown produced a string of what Chang calls "teen-targeted hip-hop exploitation flicks," including *Breakin'*, *Beat Street*, and then *Body Rock*, *Fast Forward*, and *Breakin' 2: Electric Boogaloo*.[10] These films served up a watered-down version of the culture, but they became some of the first hip hop artifacts to circulate the globe. Through both legit and bootleg copies, aspiring b-boys and b-girls everywhere saw the films, got out their cardboard strips, and in schoolyards, train stations, and on street corners they began to practice the moves.

By the mid-1980s graffiti and b-boying were in decline, and rap emerged as the central means by which hip hop culture was packaged for global consumption.[11] Run-DMC demonstrated the cross-over pop success of rap music with its cover of the rock band Aerosmith's "Walk This Way." The group earned a $1.6 million endorsement deal with Adidas, marketing the brand as part of a global hip hop lifestyle and culture. A year later Salt-N-Pepa's hit song "Push It" catapulted the female trio to worldwide fame; the song even made it to the Dutch Top 40 charts.

Cable and satellite television also played a role in disseminating rap music. In 1988 the show *Yo! MTV Raps* aired daily in the United States and soon became one of the network's first globally televised programs. It aired on MTV Europe and then MTV Asia and MTV Latino.[12] As a relatively new technology outside the United States, cable television was available mostly to privileged youth. Also, those with more disposable income were the first to consume rap music, because of their access to cassettes and videos through travel or relatives who lived abroad. It was not always true that the oppositional ideas of rap spread automatically from one marginalized segment of youth to another.

The MTV-mediated rap of the mid- to late 1980s surfaced during an era of cost-cutting deindustrialization and privatization of social services that diverted resources from America's urban centers, resulting in growing crime, gang activity, and police violence. The agitating and energetic militant rap crew Public Enemy gained tremendous popularity during this time. With berets, camouflage fatigues, and military drills reminiscent of the Black Panthers, Public Enemy revived an Afrocentric and black nationalist language that resonated with fans around the globe, from Australian Aboriginals to Samoans to black youth in South Africa, Brazil, and Tanzania. Public Enemy, a group from the black suburbs of Long Island, followed in the footsteps of Bambaataa. The group sought to take its vision of a black planet worldwide through constant touring, MTV, and multiplatinum albums.

The other trend to emerge in this era was West Coast "gangsta" rap, announcing its arrival with the defiance of NWA's "Straight Outta Compton." But, where Public Enemy was out to fight the power, gangsta rappers were concerned with survival. Where Chuck D's sense of community drew from a tradition of black protest, the community of the gangsta rapper was the 'hood. As these two currents appeared on the global stage in the era of MTV, they recalled the tension between the universal vision of Bambaataa and the ghettocentric storytelling of "The Message." How these currents would be received and riffed on at the local level remained to be seen.

By the 1990s global audiences had had access to hip hop culture for over ten years; the decade marked a period of emergence for local hip hop scenes. Rather than simply consuming American rap, global hip hoppers began to create their own versions. Like their Bronx counterparts, who developed a sound system from abandoned car radios and made turntable mixers from microphone mixers, global hip hoppers adapted materials from their local environment. They made background tracks by manually looping break beats on tape recorders. They improvised turntables with Walkmans as decks. And they relied on that most basic of technologies, the human beatbox.

The visual language of graffiti and the bodily expressions of b-boying had transcended cultural differences. But black American–accented rap in English was not so easily adapted to local contexts. Japanese rappers initially found it difficult to produce catchy rhymes because of the arrhythmic nature of their language and its positioning of the verb at the end of a sentence.[13]

Early rap outside the United States tended to imitate American rap, with performers either mimicking American rap songs or coming up with raps in English. In Tanzania, for instance, the Yo! Rap Bonanza competition, held at the New African Hotel in Dar Es Salaam in 1991, featured rappers performing in English and copying American raps. Repeating the English lyrics and copying the rhyme patterns of their favorite groups was often a way for amateur rappers to understand the flow and dissect the construction of verses.

Part of the problem was the lack of models for non-English, non-American rap. The development of bilingual rap by Latino artists in the late 1980s helped to erode the hegemony of the English language in global hip hop. In 1989 the single "Mentirosa" by the Cuban American artist Mellow Man Ace went multiplatinum. A year later the Chicano artist Kid Frost released *Hispanic Causing Panic*. Chicano rap gained popularity among youth in Latin America, particularly Colombia and Mexico. Around this time the Puerto Rican rapper Vico C, who hailed from the barrio Puerta de Tierra of San Juan, began to achieve fame with his Spanish-language rapping, and his two singles "Saborealo" and "María" went gold and platinum, respectively.

The biggest market for non-English rap in the early 1990s was in the Francophone world—covering the territories of France, West Africa, and Quebec. In 1991 the Senegalese-born French rapper MC Solaar released his debut album, *Qui Sème le Vent Récolte le Tempo* (Who Sows the Wind Reaps the Rhythm). This record went platinum, and his second album went double platinum.

The success of these French and Latino rap superstars encouraged the development of home-grown underground hip hop scenes. Local movements also began to flourish through their involvement with grassroots cultural exchanges. As a mature rap movement in the States struggled with issues of its own commodification, some rappers began to look outward to the African diaspora as a source of renewed energy.

Outside the circuit of label-organized tours, artists like Fab 5 Freddy and Paris went behind the scenes to meet with local producers, rappers, and fans. They brought their ideas, shared their techniques, donated equipment, and reported on these scenes upon their return. These cultural exchanges are situated within long histories of diasporic engagement. Global Pan-Africanism in Ghana was linked to the country's first president, Kwame Nkrumah, and visits by black intellectuals such as W. E. B. Du Bois.[14] After Bob Marley's Survival Tour of Australia and New Zealand in 1979, Australian Aboriginals began to see themselves as part of a global black movement. The Cuban revolutionary government had identified itself strongly with the black power movement in the United States and the anticolonial struggle in Africa. American civil rights and black power leaders from Stokely Carmichael to Eldridge Cleaver and Angela Davis had visited the island. But the black nationalism of contemporary hip hop artists was received with greater enthusiasm by young people feeling the effects of racism and exclusion in a new global order.

Another, more unlikely, source of support for local underground artists was the state. For a variety of reasons politicians were realizing the benefits of associating with the increasingly popular rap movements. In Cuba the revolutionary government harnessed the energy of rappers to bolster the image of Cuba as a mixed-race nation with African roots.[15] In France and Brazil municipal governments organized hip hop workshops in community centers. The Casa do Hip Hop in the *periferia* of São Paulo sponsored weekly classes in b-boying, DJ-ing, graffiti art, and rapping for neighborhood youth. The minister of culture in France under François Mitterrand brought Afrika Bambaataa over to hold hip hop seminars for young people.[16] As problems of crime and poverty spread throughout the urban peripheries in a moment of growing inequalities, culture was seen as a resource that could help divert the energies of youth to more creative pursuits while leaving the power structure intact.[17] But hip hop turned out to be a double-edged sword. It took young people off the streets while also arming them with new kinds of oppositional knowledge and the means for self-organization.

While black nationalist rap took hold in some parts of the African diaspora, in other parts gangsta rap gained momentum. Like the neighborhoods of Compton and South Central Los Angeles where gangsta originated, the barrios of Caracas, Cali, and Medellín and the townships outside Cape Town were marked by vicious cycles of poverty, incarceration, and violence. Rappers in the diaspora drew from vernacular models of masculine rebellion such as the *malandro* in Venezuela or the *tsotsi* in South Africa, in the same way that gangsta rappers in the US situated themselves within the badman tradition in African American folk culture.

Like its American counterpart, gangsta rap across the globe often consisted of first-person chronicles of ghetto life. Rappers recounted stories of being abandoned by their fathers, disappearing job prospects, and resorting to drug dealing as a means of survival. The music was also replete with references to the ghetto as a war zone, quite literally in the case of Colombia, which suffered from a long-term internal armed conflict. Gangsta rap gained immense popularity in prisons, on the streets, in the barrios. For gangsta rappers the music—like the drug trade—offered the promise of a way out of poverty.

One global icon of American gangsta rap was Tupac Shakur, whose appeal lay partly in his blending of a revolutionary ethos and "thug life." Tupacistas could be found in the favelas of Rio. Tupac murals adorned the walls of barrios in Caracas. And youth in Cape Town donned his signature bandanna.[18] Politically conscious gangsta rap was common outside the United States. The French group Suprême NTM featured a Colt .45 handgun on its album cover and used explicit language, but members of the group also denounced racial and economic exploitation.[19] Instead of using the term *gangsta*, they referred to themselves as *hard core*, a label that captured their unique melding of different genres.

Hip hop had also gained momentum outside the African diaspora during the 1990s. Hip hop culture took off in Asia. This was not surprising, as the sweatshops of hip hop fashion were in Korea, Taiwan, and China, where labels such as Ecko, Fubu, Nike, and Adidas were produced. MTV Mandarin was launched in China in 1995 and helped popularize the lifestyles and brand names of hip hop culture. At the Europe-based b-boy competition known as B-Boy Summit, crews from Japan and Korea were frequent winners, adding greater dexterity and athleticism to the form.[20]

The biggest hip hop scene in Asia was in Japan, which had a long engagement with hip hop culture and black music in general. As the anthropologist Ian Condry describes, the focus of hip hop culture in Tokyo was the club scene, and the first club devoted to hip hop appeared in 1986. A combination of company-sponsored DJ and rap competitions and tours by American artists in the late 1980s and early 1990s helped to spur the nascent rap scene.[21] Although Japanese record labels were reluctant to release rap music at this time, it had a growing following among youth. Japanese hip hop fans have been criticized for consuming black culture as a fad with little knowledge of black history.[22] While the picture is more complex than this— some Japanese artists and fans do make an attempt to learn about black culture and history—the debate does point to the uneasy place of Asians within the Global Hip Hop Nation.[23]

Hip hop has been highly popular not just in Asia but also among Asian immigrant youth in Western nations such as Canada, Australia, Britain, and the United States. But Asians are not a homogeneous group. The forebears of long-standing communities of working-class Asians in the Caribbean, Pacific Islands, northeastern Australia, and East Africa arrived as indentured laborers during the colonial period. In Britain, working-class South Asians, along with Caribbean immigrants, have historically identified as black Britons because of a shared history of racist exclusion. This has led to the idea of an "Afro-Asian Atlantic" that recognizes the diasporic engagements between blacks, Asians, and Arabs.[24] British South Asian rap groups such as Fundamental that identify as black are therefore locating themselves within this specific history.

In contrast, Asians emigrating to the United States since 1965 have tended to be upper middle class. The dominant image of Asian Americans as upwardly mobile or "model minorities" has placed them at odds with blacks and Latinos. One notable exception is Filipino Americans, who often share the circumstances of urban blacks and Latinos in places like the West Coast. They have been prominent as b-boys and DJs in West Coast hip hop.[25] But the majority of middle-class Asian American consumers of rap tend to inhabit a position similar to affluent whites in the suburbs and have little contact with racialized poverty.

By the mid- to late 1990s the market for global hip hop was being recognized by the music industry, and many local acts had achieved commercial success. The first rap hit in Japan came in 1994, when Scha Dara Parr's single "Boogie Back Tonight" went platinum. Following two more platinum singles in 1995, by the rap group East End X Yuri, the industry coined the term *J-rap*. The Cuban rap group Orishas sold 400,000 copies of its debut album in 1998 after signing to EMI and went on to win two Grammys. These successes, echoed in other contexts as well, created a greater visibility for global hip hop. But such popularity also led to a growing divide, between groups that called themselves underground—rejecting fusion with other genres and maintaining a political stance—and commercial groups that geared their music toward mass audiences to gain industry acceptance. The divide between underground and commercial was not always clearly drawn. But it did reflect real contests over access to resources as multinational corporations entered the field and sought to exploit the industry potential of local scenes.

The year 1996 was a watershed for rap. On February 8, 1996, President Bill Clinton signed the Telecommunications Act, which relaxed media ownership rules. The legislation accompanied broader neoliberal policies of privatization and deregulation. Before passage of the measure a company could not own more than two radio stations in a single market. But as a result of the removal of ownership caps, companies were allowed to own up to seven or eight stations.

The Future of Music Coalition estimated that by 2001 ten companies controlled about two-thirds of the airwaves as a result of the Telecommunications Act. The biggest media conglomerate to emerge from this process was Clear Channel Communications. It owned twelve hundred commercial stations in 2002.[26] By the start of the new millennium, 80 percent of the music industry was controlled by five companies—Vivendi Universal, Sony, AOL Time Warner, Bertelsmann, and EMI.[27] The post-1996 period after the Telecommunications Act was passed came to be seen as the era of corporate rap. The airwaves were dominated by a catchy pop formula coming from a handful of producers.

This trend toward big radio has been followed across the globe. While local scenes had matured and developed, many radio stations were playing mostly American rap. In Kenya the radio stations Capital FM and KISS FM program American artists like 50 Cent because, they argue, it helps corporations sell their products.[28] It is clear that corporate rap on the radio is designed to exploit a lucrative youth market. This American-dominated radio programming contrasts somewhat with television's practices—about half the programming on MTV Base Africa is African, and about 70 percent of MTV Mandarin's videos are Chinese. At the same time television has been an important medium for promoting hip hop lifestyles and commodities. In Beijing, McDonald's has produced a commercial using Mandarin rap. Likewise, Pepsi, Sprite, and China Mobile have all used rap in their China ads.[29] But rap does not just advertise products. The content of rap songs is so heavily brand identified—from cars to clothing and alcohol—that the music becomes fused with the product. Hip hop has raised the sales of Hennessy cognac by so much that the French company sponsored a contest and offered as the prize a visit to its plant with a famous rapper.[30] It is clear that the innovation and creativity that gave rise to hip hop culture were not to be found in the realm of corporate rap.

The global spread of corporate rap, combined with its popularity among white suburban consumers in the United States, produced troubling racial contradictions for the genre. S. Craig Watkins suggests that corporate rap was designed with young white consumers in mind and that the fascination of white and suburban youth with rap music was just a more complex expression of racism.[31] This was particularly notable in the global arena. American rap acts on tour frequently encountered all-white audiences. The Aboriginal rapper Wire MC recounts the chilling experience of being at a 50 Cent concert in Sydney and seeing the packed white male audience chanting, "Put another cap in a nigga."[32] In some cases local rap artists misappropriated rap's oppositional language to openly reassert racial hierarchies. The commercially popular Israeli rappers Subliminal and The Shadow used their music to advance a right-wing Zionist agenda. The rappers identified with the Israeli army, justifying the occupation of Palestine and presenting themselves as the underdogs.[33]

One response to the dominance of corporate rap on the airwaves was the development of an underground rap movement in the United States between 1995 and 1999. As independent and underground emcees found themselves with less access to major labels, radio airtime, and venues, they began to find alternative means to build a fan base. The Internet became an important resource as a digital distribution network in challenging the power of the traditional record labels. College and community radio stations offered more varied playlists than the corporate radio stations.[34] And the DIY (do-it-yourself) model—selling tapes out of the trunk as a way to move to a regional label and then a major label—began to be used by underground artists.

The genre of underground rap allowed for a greater variety of narratives than the highly commodified and one-dimensional corporate rap. But, with American underground rap, the locus of hip hop moved away from urban, black, and working-class sectors as artists and audiences became increasingly middle class, white, and multiracial.[35] Underground rap in the US paralleled the rise of underground rap abroad, and underground artists in diverse contexts often shared a suspicion of fusing rap and other musical forms, although the artists didn't always have a common political stance.

Local place-based hip hop genres also began to emerge in cities across the US, from the San Francisco Bay Area's "hyphy" culture to southern "crunk" and New Orleans "bounce" music, the latter influenced by brass band sound and Mardi Gras Indian chants. Greater regionalization of rap began to take place in other countries, too. In France, for instance, unique rap movements emerged in Marseilles and Strasbourg.[36] Regionalization was matched by the growing diversity of sounds and styles in global hip hop. These included the rap-reggae-traditional blend of kwaito in South Africa, the popular highlife rap mix of hiplife music in Ghana, and the drum 'n' bass-, garage-influenced Brit-hop in Britain. Local scenes also diversified, incorporating reggae rap, gangsta rap, spoken-word rap, hard-core rap, rock rap, and R&B-influenced rap under the broader umbrella of hip hop culture. By 2000 hip hop had become a global tour de force, marking out terrain in both mass culture—where its dominant appeal lay—and on the level of the subcultures—where its real dynamism resided.

Like Afrika Bambaataa in the 1980s and Public Enemy in the 1990s, the Black August Hip Hop Project emerged to spread its message of a united hip hop globe in the new millennium. Black August was a network established during the 1970s in the California prison system as a way of linking up movements for resistance in the Americas. The hip hop collective sought to draw connections between radical black activism and hip hop culture. In its statement of purpose, the collective defined its goals as "support[ing] the global development of hip hop culture by facilitating exchanges between international communities where hip hop is a vital part of youth culture, and by promoting awareness about the social and political issues that affect these youth communities."[37] The collective arranged for the American emcees Paris, Common, dead prez, Tony Touch, Mos Def, and Talib Kweli to perform at the annual Cuban hip hop festivals in Alamar during the late 1990s. In 2001 it organized a concert at the World Conference against Racism in Durban and proposed a tour of South Africa that again would include Kweli and dead prez, as well as Black Thought, Boots Riley, and Jeru the Damaja.

Just like the hip hop ambassadors who preceded them, the Black August rappers were met abroad with a sense of great expectation and enthusiasm. Their language of black nationalism resonated with Cuban and South African youths feeling the effects of racial discrimination as their once-radical leaders pursued policies of austerity. The Cuban emcee Sekou Umoja, from the group Anónimo Consejo, told me, "We had the same vision as rappers such as Paris, who was one of the first to come to Cuba. His music drew my attention, because here is something from the barrio, something black. Of blacks, and made principally by blacks, which in a short time became something very much our own, related to our lives here in Cuba." The rapper Common organized a meeting with local rappers at which they exchanged ideas and stories. The Black August network brought equipment and records for the Cuban rappers. But, as occurred with the electrifying performances of Bambaataa and Chuck D, it was in the concerts that Black August's vision of transnational solidarity was realized. The chants of "I'm an African," led by dead prez in Alamar, thundered through the stadium as Afro-Cuban youth defiantly claimed their black roots.

The pain of racism may have been the bridge that connected the American rappers with those in the diaspora. But that racism took different forms in each context. On stage in Alamar dead prez burned a dollar bill as a symbol of American capitalism, horrifying local audiences, who saw it as a week's worth of bread. In South Africa the American artists came to protest the racism of their own government, which withdrew from the Durban conference along with Israel. Yet when the American artists left the concert stage to return to their fancy hotels, the affinities broke down. The American artists' treatment of leading local artists as hired drivers left a sense that racism looked different for the privileged Americans.[38] Frustrated with this disrespect, the local promoters canceled the tour. Not the least of the problems was the American artists' clichéd notions of African-ness. The cover of dead prez's album *lets get free* featured militant black women raising guns to the sky. While dead prez claimed that the image was from the Soweto Uprising in 1976, South African hip hoppers knew that it was from the war of independence.[39]

The attempt to foster cultural exchange and understanding instead drew claims of cultural imperialism from local emcees. Global hip hop scenes were now about twenty years old, and they had their own stars and styles. All that local rappers wanted was to be treated as equals by the visiting American rappers. But, clearly, there were hierarchies within global hip hop. And while Black August saw its mission as promoting social consciousness, some South African rappers saw it as Americans conquering Africa with their rhymes and coming to save the Africans.[40] Other local rappers saw a gap between the politically committed lyrics of the Black August rappers and their actions. As the Cuban rapper Soandry, then of the duo Hermanos de Causa, told the documentary filmmakers Vanessa and Larissa Díaz, "It's not saying it, it's not singing it, it's showing it. To me—none of these people, not dead prez, not Common Sense,[41] not Mos Def have shown me anything. They just say what they say in their songs, but they don't represent that."[42] Soandry was also bitter about the various rap collaborations between visiting American rappers and Cuban rappers. The resulting productions tended to make money for the American artists but not the Cubans. Cuban rappers, South African rappers, and others were getting tired of the one-way stream of Westerners who were treating local scenes in Cuba, South Africa, and elsewhere as exotic cultures to be packaged for the consumption of Western audiences.

In 1999 the Venezuelan producer Juan Carlos Echeandía decided to make a documentary film that looked at American hip hop. It was the first time a producer from the South—albeit a relatively privileged one—had traveled to the States to interview American artists, producers, and fans. Echeandía returned to Venezuela and documented the growing underground hip hop scene there as well. The result was *Venezuela subterránea: cuatro elementos, una música* (Underground Venezuela: Four Elements, One Music). The film was low budget. The dissemination was not large. But the idea that a hip hopper from the global south might have something to say about American hip hop destabilized the idea that Americans were the ultimate authority on all hip hop, including their own.

By the new millennium, the divide between American and non-American rappers was becoming somewhat irrelevant as diasporic rappers came on the scene. As global hip hop began to come of age, hip hoppers found themselves increasingly torn between the need to make a living and the desire to pursue their art. With record labels picking off a scant few to sign and promote, the rest were left to wonder where their lives were headed. For many, pursuing a career in music meant leaving the comfort of their local scene and heading to international cities. Local superstars in Brazil or Kenya became busboys in New York or taxi drivers in London in order to pursue their dreams. The other source of diasporic hip hop was second generation immigrants from Haiti, Somalia, and Egypt, among other places; these young people were beginning to find a political voice through hip hop. As artists and fans, they generated new circuits of performance, activism, and solidarity that brought into question the fixed national boundaries that had defined hip hop scenes.

In some ways hip hop has been both global and diasporic since its beginnings. Hip hop's lineage includes the West African griots, or professional singers. It has strong roots in Jamaican dance hall music, itself a mélange of different musical influences. Several founders of hip hop culture were Caribbean immigrants: DJ Kool Herc was Jamaican and Grandmaster Flash was from Barbados. B-boying draws on influences as varied as Brazilian capoeira and East Asian karate films. Even today American rap songs incorporate global cultural forms, from Bollywood film songs and Rastafarian religions to Tahitian dance styles. The global is at the heart of hip hop culture, which from the start has borrowed and appropriated and sampled from cultures around the world.

But the diasporic rap of the new millennium emerged in a unique context—that of the post 9/11 world. The terrorist attacks of September 11, 2001, drastically reshaped the contours of race, politics, and global war. The world became embroiled in a "war against terrorism," in which those perceived as "against us" were often Muslims and people of color. Arab and South Asian immigrant communities were seen as the internal enemy. The children of immigrants born and raised their whole lives in the United States, Australia, France, England, or elsewhere were made to feel like outsiders.

Diasporic hip hop has forged a new global politics of solidarity that connects racism against African Americans to anti-Arab profiling in urban areas and links these issues to the occupation in Palestine and the war in Iraq. Palestinian American emcees such as the Michigan-based Iron Sheik challenge the erasure and denial of Palestinian histories in American public discourse. As the anthropologist Sunana Maira recounts, diasporic rappers have come together in cross-national collaborations such as the 2007 Arab Summit, a project that includes the Palestinian American rapper Excentrik, Ragtop from the Filipino-Palestinian-American group the Philistines, the Syrian American rapper Omar Offendum from the NOMADS, and the Iraqi-Canadian rapper Narcicyst from the trio Euphrates. These kinds of collaboration are rooted in cross-ethnic activist alliances of black activists from hurricane-stricken New Orleans, Palestinian activists demanding a right to return, and people opposed to the militarization of the US-Mexico border and the apartheid wall in Palestine.[43] For British rappers, such as the South Asian Muslim groups Kaliphz and Fundamental, criticisms of local racism and the global war on terror are couched in the language of militant Islam.[44] At a time when Islam has replaced black power as the enemy within, it's not surprising that it has reemerged as a possible axis for solidarity in the hip hop globe.

Rap has provided a means for young people from immigrant communities to break the silence and network with others locally and globally. And these youth have become the latest hip hop ambassadors to emerge. The Liberian American Blade Brown raps about building a Pan-African consciousness, and in his rhymes he connects racism and slavery to the poverty of many African nations. Although based in the Twin Cities, Blade's producer is from Tanzania, and Blade has collaborated with other diasporic artists in the Twin Cities such as the Kenyan American MC Baraka.[45] African emigration to places like the Twin Cities, Toronto, and New York is creating alternative spaces that break down national boundaries.

Four generations of hip hop ambassadors have traversed the globe with the desire to transcend their immediate realities and link up with others through a universal politics of justice. This communitarian strand of hip hop culture now exists as a counterpoint to the grossly materialistic, individualist nature of corporate rap. But it has sat uneasily alongside the storytellers of the genre, who have been concerned not so much with grand gestures as with rap as a chronicle of everyday life.

In its most contemporary manifestation, hip hop again faced the incongruity of the desire for unity and fellowship across borders and the need to be grounded in a specific place and experience. Diasporic rappers didn't draw the same charges of cultural imperialism that earlier rappers did; first-generation immigrants in particular were deeply rooted in the cultures and histories that had produced local scenes. But, as their years in the diaspora went by, it became harder for these artists to maintain a bridge with their past. Their concerns were now different from those issues they had left behind. Unmoored from place, they were in danger of losing touch with the specificity at the heart of their music. The Cuban DJ Ariel Fernández, who emigrated to New York City in 2005, posed this question: "Cuban rap doesn't have the same value outside of its context. It was made in Cuba and for Cubans. How will the movement continue with the same importance outside of Cuba? We cannot pursue it with the same time and energy. And there is not a big public for Cuban immigrant rap."[46] It has been difficult for rappers as new immigrants to pursue their art, given the demands of everyday survival. They don't have the same sense of being part of a movement, now that they are scattered in different cities and often separated from their group members. Without the realities of place to anchor it, a politics of global solidarity might start to sound hollow. And at its core hip hop has always been about bearing witness.

In the pages that follow I trace some of the paths that have been carved out by hip hop culture across the globe. I do not intend to provide an exhaustive history of global hip hop or even a summary of national/regional hip hop scenes. Rather, I take readers on my own kind of global tour, through the cities where I have lived, the artists I have met, and the insights I have gleaned. This book is not a who's who of global hip hop's celebrities and icons. It brings the narratives of well-known artists together with those of lesser-known artists—what they have in common is my great respect for their work and my belief that their stories deserve to be told.

What drives my travels is the same question that has motivated the hip hop ambassadors of each generation: What is it about hip hop that connects young and marginalized people around the globe? In addition to my physical trip from Sydney to Havana, Chicago, and Caracas, the book documents my personal journey as I struggle with my own commitment to hip hop as an activist and as an artist. In the mid-1990s I formed a rap group with an Aboriginal woman and a Pacific Islander man in Sydney. But, as I compared their lives and my own, I often wondered how I could justify my participation in a genre dominated by narratives of deprivation. Rap was more than a vehicle for political messages—it was a way of giving voice to the shared experiences of a community. But *which* community did I belong to, and *whose* voice was I trying to represent? I encountered these questions again and again during my travels as I sought affinities with revolutionary rappers in Havana, Asian Americans in Chicago, and blackfullas (Aboriginal people) in Sydney.

Close to the Edge betrays my fleeting hope that there is something that connects a global generation of young people, born in an era when corporate-led globalization undermined their basic standard of living yet deprived them of the tools to protest. Whereas their parents' generation took to the streets, they took up a microphone. The rapid-fire spread of the culture was more than media hype. The appeal was more than a fad. Something in the drums spoke to barrio youth in Medellín, French teenagers in the cités, blackfullas in Sydney's Inner West, and young people in the townships outside Cape Town. And something spoke to me.

CHAPTER ONE

Made in Havana City

A re you Latina?" Clad in a khaki green safari suit, the immigration official at José Martí International Airport in Havana peered at me over the top of thick rimmed glasses as he examined my passport.

"No." It seemed best to keep things brief.

"So why does it say here that your name is Fernandes?"

I trotted out the usual response. "Because my parents are from the part of India in the South that was colonized by the Portuguese." So much for brevity.

His brow wrinkled. "But this is an Australian passport."

"Yes, my parents migrated from India to Australia thirty years ago, and I was born there. I'm an Australian citizen."

"So why are you coming to Cuba?"

Why was an Australian-born, Indian-descended, Portuguese-surnamed gringa like me coming to Cuba? Would you believe, to deliver pickles? On my mother's orders I was bringing home-made dried shrimp pickle for my sister Deepa. Deepa, who had lived in the Ecuadorian forests with shamans and hitch-hiked down the Amazon with another adventurous soul, was now a features producer at Radio Habana, and our mother's main concern was, "Is she eating properly?" I had successfully smuggled the jar of pickle through Tokyo and Montreal in my circuitous route to Havana, and it was only in Mexico City that a scrutinizing customs official asked me to open it. The thought of disrobing the bulky jar—swaddled by my mum in layers of plastic and tape—was so ludicrous that I burst into hysterical laughter. The Mexican official, taken aback at first, joined me in laughing and sent me on my way with the jar untouched.

This official before me now wasn't laughing. It seemed best to keep things brief. "I'm visiting my sister."

My covert mission as a pickle courier aside, I figured that this was my opportunity to see revolution in action. It was January 1998, and I had finally graduated from college after years of part-time study. I had spent my undergraduate years as a student activist trying to convince other students that capitalism was unjust, and, if we wanted to know what a true socialist society might be like, we should look to Cuba. My bible was a booklet called *The Cuban Revolution and Its Extension*, which lauded the bold and radical revolution carried out on this small Caribbean island. I argued passionately with the student conservatives and anarchists who said that Cuba's was an authoritarian society where citizen rights were restricted and homosexuals were locked up. Of course, I was aware that Cuba had its problems. But I also felt that the Western media painted a distorted picture of what was really happening on the island. I had read the auto-biography of the former Black Panther Angela Davis, and, like her, I imagined myself joining the masses to cut sugarcane in the fields.

As an aspiring emcee, I had heard that Cuban hip hop was the site of a rebirth of revolutionary rap music. All kinds of American rappers, from the indie star Common to the rapper-turned-actor Mos Def, had come down here to perform at the annual hip hop festival. In her emails from Havana, Deepa described in detail all the rappers and producers she was meeting and told me she could introduce me to them. I was intrigued. What did hip hop look like in this place where revolution had such a potent meaning and history? Hip hop was known as a revolutionary music, as a culture of protest, but what would hip hop be in a country like Cuba, where the state itself was said to be revolutionary? Could it be a *counter*revolutionary force here?

Cuba seemed the ideal place to continue my journey in search of a global hip hop generation. My exploration had begun in Sydney, where I joined in workshops for a hip hop theatrical production on Sydney's West Side. But as I watched hip hop in Sydney being taken over by mainstream record labels, I wondered if I might find a purer, more authentic, form of the culture in Cuba. What would it be like in a place that had not been infiltrated by Americanization? I was curious about how a digital age music like hip hop had developed such deep roots in a metropolitan city that had only two Internet cafes. What could it tell us about the power of hip hop as a truly global form?

There's no time to sleep," said Deepa, as she climbed into the back of the powder blue 1952 Chevrolet. "We've only got an hour to drop off your bags and make it to the rumba."

Our driver sped along Boyeros, the long road from the airport to the city, and headed for the tree-lined suburb of El Vedado. Deepa helped me lug my bags up the flight of stairs to the *casa particular*, a private home where she was renting a room from a Cuban couple with a teenage daughter. My sleep-deprived body longed for the bed with its fresh sheets. Outside the driver beeped his horn impatiently.

"C'mon," prodded Deepa, sensing I was weakening. "There'll be plenty of time for sleep later."

The National Writers and Artists Union, known locally by its acronym, UNEAC, was at the corner of Calle 17 and H in El Vedado. There was a rumba on its lawns every Wednesday afternoon. At the gates of the mansion that housed UNEAC, a young man sat collecting money.

"Don't say anything, just follow me," Deepa instructed, as we approached the front of the line. She handed him a ten-peso note and he let us in.

"What was that about?" I asked her, once we were inside the gates.

"Cubans pay in pesos, foreigners pay in dollars." She indicated a blond woman at the gate, who was fishing out a five-dollar bill.

Cuba faced a severe crisis after the collapse of its main benefactor, the Soviet Union, in 1991. Anticipating internal unrest in

Cuba, the US had tightened the screws of its three-decade economic embargo, making life even more difficult on the island. The Cuban government christened these years the "Special Period." The dual peso-dollar economy had developed in the early nineties as a strategy to help the economy recover. After years of being seen as contraband, the dollar was now recognized as legal tender. Dollars entered through remittances from Florida, tourists on vacation, and money earned abroad. But Cubans still earned in pesos. With an exchange rate of twenty-one pesos to the dollar, we had paid just twenty-five cents each to get in. That was the same as Cubans would pay. Deepa was being paid in pesos by Radio Habana, so she was entitled to the peso rate. But she didn't even need to produce ID. No one here suspected we were foreigners. This was one of the perks of looking Cuban.

There were a hundred or so people gathered on the lawns of UNEAC. Foreigners and Cubans, kids and their parents, and older people resting in the shade all waited for the show to begin. Salsa came from speakers on the stage. A few well-dressed young Cuban men mingled with the French and Scandinavian tourists. The Cubans swiveled their hips effortlessly. Their fluid steps and graceful turns contrasted with the jerky and self-conscious movements of their partners.

"*Jineteros.*" Deepa nodded her head toward the young men. "It literally means 'jockey,' but here in Cuba they use it to refer to street hustlers and sex workers."

"But I thought that prostitution was illegal here." I recalled reading that the revolutionary government had outlawed prostitution in 1961. Thousands of women who had been involved in the sex trade during the prerevolutionary era were introduced to other occupations through work-study programs and vocational schools.

"Well, nowadays most Cubans find it hard to make ends meet," replied Deepa. "Prostitution is just another way to survive." Next to me, a young white man in a Che t-shirt snuggled with a pretty Cubana with light brown skin and curly hair. Were they girlfriend and boyfriend? Was she a *jinetera*? How could you tell?

A half hour or so later, just as my lids were beginning to droop again, an announcement was made. The rap act Primera Base would be making an appearance. Sometimes rappers opened for the main acts at the rumba.

"Primera Base. Cool!" Deepa said in anticipation. "They're one of Cuba's most well-known rap groups, and they even have a disc out with EGREM." EGREM was the state agency responsible for producing and marketing Cuban music. With scarce resources and a small local market for CD sales, EGREM had produced only a few rap CDs. They received little or no airplay on Cuban radio.

I strained my neck to get a good view of the stage. Three young men stood before the microphones. The one in the middle, Rubén Maning, had several thick gold chains around his neck. His shirt was open to reveal a bare torso. He wore plastic sunglasses studded with fake diamonds. Low-slung pants revealed a pair of white boxers with the letter X written in bold at the top. The other two also wore heavy gold chains and black sunglasses.

"It was like this," opened Rubén, in a grave voice. He bowed his head dramatically. "The 21 of February 1965, he was shot up in the Audubon Ballroom / About to give his last speech, before an auditorium of 400 blacks and half a dozen whites / Yes! That gentleman you know as Malcolm X / WAS DEAD." From the recorded background beat came the piercing tones of a siren, then people screaming and crying. The beat kicked in, and Rubén performed an homage to Malcolm X. "I want to be a black just like you, with your great virtue," rapped Rubén, in an old-school flow. "I want to be a black just like you, a great leader, to be great." The symbol of Malcolm was so powerful, I thought.

"Just like you, just like you, nigger," Primera Base went on to rap in the chorus. "We wanna be a nigger like you / Just like you, just like you, nigger. A nigger like you."

I sighed. Also powerful was the circulation of the N-word in a global marketplace. It made me wonder whether Cuban rappers were just a tropical version of white American kids in the suburbs, using black slang and getting their bling on. Were we just looking at the mirror image of a clichéd American commercial culture? And all this in a country that was supposed to be the last holdout against American global influence? Or maybe I was just looking in the wrong places.

Early hip hop culture in Cuba was generally produced and consumed in the local neighborhood. During this period of the late 1980s through the mid-1990s, people would play music from CDs brought from the United States. Rappers would rhyme in their houses, on street corners, and in local parks. When I arrived in Cuba in 1998, this local culture was still strong, even as hip hop was gaining ground in the clubs and venues like UNEAC. Randy Acosta was a rapper who began his career on the streets of his barrio, Almendares, a few miles from the center of the city. I went with Deepa to visit him and his mother, Lily. I thought that Randy might give me a sense of how Cuban hip hop looked from the streets. I figured we would take a taxi or a bus to get there. Deepa had other ideas.

"We're hitchhiking," she informed me once we were out on the street.

After the cult thriller *The Hitcher*, I thought no one hitchhiked anymore. In Havana not only did people hitchhike, but hitchhiking was enforced by the baton-wielding police. Few Cubans were privileged to own cars. Those who did were mostly people with a dollar income from tourism or those who worked for a joint venture. Even then there was the gas shortage. The Soviet Union used to be Cuba's main oil supplier, but in 1990 the Soviets just stopped delivering oil. Cuba's transportation system was paralyzed. As the economy picked up slowly again, those with advantages were forced to share. Making sure that every car was full of passengers was one way of keeping things moving.

Deepa and I walked over to the intersection of Linea and Paseo to *coger botella*, as hitchhiking was known locally. Cubans refer to a ride as a *botella,* or bottle. So to *coger botella* was to get a ride. Deepa stuck out her thumb, true hitchhiker style. But when a red Volkswagen spluttered to a halt before us, the police officer directing traffic came over and bent down to speak to the driver. "Are you going to Playa?" he asked the driver, a thin older man in a pink shirt. "Yes," was the response. "Then you can take them." He motioned us toward the car. Legally enforced carpooling. Only in Cuba, I thought as we drove toward the tunnel to Miramar. In a revolutionary society solutions were collective and relied on people's sense of obligation to others. And maybe some fear of the baton-wielding cops as well.

When we arrived at her house, Lily was watching her TV—a Russian model with a greenish hue to the screen. In the 1980s Lily had gone to Czechoslovakia to work with Cuban delegations. She spoke fluent Czech, another of those skills of little use in an era of Canadian and French joint ventures. She was a single mother who supported her son, Randy, on her peso salary from her job at an advertising agency.

As we chatted over thick Cuban coffee and *mani*, a popular sweet made from palm sugar and peanuts, Randy walked in. He pulled off his bicycle helmet and shot us a broad smile just like his mother's. He tentatively pulled back a chair to sit down with us. As Randy talked about his passion for rap, he became more animated. He told us that he had always identified with rap, with its cadence and the drums. It was hard to find American music in Cuba. So he mostly watched bootleg recordings of video clips on friends' VCRs.

His shyness dissipated, Randy performed his rap song "La Bicicleta" (The Bicycle). The song was about the scarcity of transportation and his journeys around the city on his Chinese-made Flying Pigeon bicycle. Randy's five-year-old cousin Cesarito—who had memorized the words—repeated the lyrics and chimed in with a childlike attempted beatbox. As I looked on, it all seemed so familiar: the rhythms, the hand gestures, the flow. But what he was rapping about was entirely unfamiliar, a scene taken from the tableau of his own life and told in the vernacular of his peers.

The early gender politics of Cuban hip hop—like the race politics that I had witnessed with Primera Base—were still underdeveloped. As in most places around the world, the culture of machismo in Cuba was strong. As an ardent feminist, I was taken aback by the whistles and propositions that I, like most women, attracted from street-corner types. After years of organizing protest marches to mark International Women's Day in Sydney, I was surprised to hear that on this day in Cuba women were handed roses and congratulated for being women. So would Cuban hip hop be any different? Deepa's friend Pablo Herrera, Cuba's most prominent hip hop producer, took us to a *peña*, a small afternoon rap show at the local Café Cantante. He said that we would see and meet some of the prominent women artists in Cuban hip hop.

Café Cantante was a small intimate venue facing the historic Plaza de la Revolución. We descended a series of marble stairs to the entrance, where we paid—yet again—five pesos each and then made our way into the club. Like most other venues struggling to survive the economic crisis, Café Cantante had to reorient itself toward a tourist market. Evening concerts that showcased top Cuban bands such as NG La Banda and Irakere cost upward of $25 per ticket, almost twice the monthly salary of a Cuban. The afternoons were when young Cubans had a chance to use the space, for rap or rock concerts.

"Respect! All crew, all massive, everywhere in the world / You practice the art of hip hop / This goes out to every boy and every girl." Ariel Fernández, aka DJ Asho, was spinning, and the cramped space vibrated with the booming voice of KRS-One. At a table by the front of the crowded room sat a tall stick-thin guy and a reticent young black woman with springy brass-colored hair. Pablo introduced them as Alexey Rodríguez and Magia López, a husband-wife rap duo known as Obsesión.

"¿Voy a cantar?" I asked Magia in my beginner's Spanish, misconjugating my verbs so that I was requesting to sing rather than asking if they would be singing, as I'd intended. "Si, un momento." She conferred with someone at the back and then came back to announce that I had been added to the afternoon's lineup. Oh, shit! I tried to explain the mix-up but to no avail.

On stage first was Instinto, the all-female trio extraordinaire. The women were dressed in low-cut and clingy outfits and high heels. As the salsa beat kicked in from the DJ booth, they gyrated their hips in a choreographed routine. The young men in the audience went wild. The divas onstage rapped in lyrical prose, spun on their heels, and sang in three-part harmony. This was the Cuban-streets-meet-high-brow-classical-training at Havana's Instituto Superior de Arte. There was no way I could match a performance like this. Was it too late to get out of it?

Then the next act was being introduced, a Portuguese rapper from India. Heads, including my own, turned in anticipation of this exotic wonder until I realized they were talking about me. Too late. I smoothed down my blue jeans and hesitantly edged onto the stage. I had no slinky dress. I had no background beat. And, worst of all, I was performing solo. If there was an unspoken rule among Cuban rappers, it was that you always perform with one or more others—you never brave the stage alone. I could feel the collective gasp of shock as I came onto the stage—by myself.

I decided to sing one of my new pieces, "Woman Find." The fast and scatlike rhymes were inspired by the jazz–hip hop fusion style of the LA-based rap group Freestyle Fellowship. I realized I would be totally incomprehensible to a Cuban audience. The song was a militant tract about women breaking beyond stereotypes and finding a voice in society. As I sang the chorus, "We'll no more believe when they tell us we're free," Alexey and some others added improvised timbals with a spoon on the side of a glass. There were a few cheers and some scattered clapping when I finished. I figured that somehow, despite the language barriers, maybe the song had resonated among some people. As I walked down off the stage and back to my seat, I felt hands on my arm. "Que linda." "Que guapa." I was being surrounded by young men who liked my pretty song.

I sighed, deflated, and took my seat. "That was alright," said Pablo, leaning over from his seat. "Maybe I can produce some music for you."

Pablo lived in Santos Suárez, a formerly middle-class area in the southern part of the city now occupied by working-class blacks. It wasn't until my next trip to Cuba, after spending a year and a half at grad school in Chicago, that I finally made it to Pablo's place. I was curious about how rap music graduated from barrios like Almendares to the recording studios. If most of Cuba ran on old Soviet equipment, how did Cubans acquire the samplers and mixers and other expensive equipment required to make beats? A beat was the prerecorded background music that accompanied rappers as they performed. It had replaced the records played by DJs in early live rap performances.

I caught a cab to the modest two-story corner house that Pablo shared with his mother. There was a rich aroma of tomatoes. Pablo was cooking pasta. A sauce simmered on one burner, noodles on the other, and eggs boiled in another pan. After draining the noodles and dishing them into bowls with the sauce, he peeled the boiled eggs and crumbled them on top. Pablo saw the look on my face.

"I know, it's weird," he admitted, in his disarmingly impeccable English. "It's just another habit from the Special Period. Cheese was so hard to come by, and we Cubans are always *inventando*, so we just substituted it with crumbled up eggs. Try it, it actually tastes pretty good!"

I sampled the local cuisine. The pasta sauce was tasty. I figured if I ever got caught in a special period, I'd just do without the cheese.

After we ate and cleaned up the dishes, we went into Pablo's studio. It was a tiny room next to the kitchen. There was a Roland keyboard sampler, a Behringer mixing board, a microphone shielded by a homemade pop screen made of panty hose, a set of turntables, and—he showed me proudly—an Akai MPC digital sampler that had been sent by a US label that August. Pablo read the manual in English. In only ten days of working with the equipment, he had produced the first-ever Cuban hip hop album. It was called *Cuban Hip Hop All-Stars, Vol. 1*.

"We're lucky to have equipment like this, because of our connections with record labels," Pablo said, gesturing toward the sampler. "But we always have to make it clear that we reject the kind of consumerist ethic and materialism that drives hip hop as an industry. Like a few weeks ago, a photographer from *Vibe* magazine wanted to do a shoot of Cuban rappers wearing Tommy Hilfiger. We refused, because we knew that it was just an attempt by labels to get their products into Cuba."

I nodded. Rappers were wary of being accused of "capitalist consumerism," a desire for material goods that was at odds with being a revolutionary. Foreign labels—even underground ones—were capitalist corporations that tempted the rappers with record deals and expensive, hard-to-acquire equipment. Cuban rappers and foreign labels were engaged in a *rumba guaguancó*. They flirted with one another, each enticing the other while protecting themselves. The courtship worked only if both parties thought that they were using the other for their own ends.

The sampler was a godsend for Cuban hip hoppers. Until that moment they had just made do with whatever materials were available to them. For improvised backgrounds Cubans made "pause tapes." They would record the break beat on a cassette and then manually loop it over and over until they had a complete song.

Cuba's first hip hop DJ, Ariel Fernández, improvised a set of turntables with Walkmans as the decks. His cassettes contained music recorded from CDs and FM stations. At *bonches*, the block parties, or local gatherings in the barrio, Ariel would set up two Walkmans. He would play a cassette in one Walkman while searching for the song he wanted on the other. Then he would flip to the other song. He didn't have a mixer that would allow a seamless transition from one song to the next, but he made do with volume controls. The important thing was, as he said, to preserve the principle of the turntables.[1] It was yet another example of the creative spirit of *inventando*.

The MPC in the hands of Pablo meant that rappers who worked with him could now actually have beats that used Cuban rhythms and samples. I pulled out the lyrics for my rap song "You're My Shadow," and I sang a few lines for Pablo. It was a song about heartbreak and betrayal, and the comfort one could find in female friendships. Pablo pondered it for a minute. He extracted an old Cuban bolero record by Blanca Rosa Gil from his vinyl collection, put it on the decks, and sampled one line from the track "Acerca el oido" (Bring your ears closer). "Dejame contarte el olvido, Dejame decirte el olvido" (Let me tell you the forgotten, Let me say to you the forgotten). The sample added a plaintive suggestion of memory, perhaps an older voice imparting wisdom to a younger person. Pablo recorded this phrase on the MPC, along with a drum loop and a bass line. Turning to the keyboard, he began tapping out a few simple melodies. He finally settled on a quick ascending triplet that led into the melody and then a three-note riff that played off the bass line. He copied these to the sampler, too. Pleased with the beat so far, he sampled an alluring female voice saying, "Escuchala" (Hear it) from another album. He added the sample with a jarring syncopation slightly after the end of the phrase.

Afterward Pablo walked me out to the street to flag down a cab. He slipped on an Ecko t-shirt with the words "Ecko Unltd, NYC" printed on the front. He looked at me sheepishly. "An American producer was here last week, and he offered me all this clothing. I wouldn't have taken it, but I really needed some new clothes."

Maybe protesting capitalist consumerism was just a luxury for those of us in the West. Here in Cuba sometimes necessity had to come first. With clothing hard to find or priced in dollars at the fancy Carlos Tercera shopping mall, hip hoppers like Pablo couldn't always turn down the offerings of the foreign labels. And, no doubt, Pablo knew that turning up at the next block party in an Ecko t-shirt would turn some heads.

Cuba seemed not to be as isolated from global music trends as I had thought. Producers, tourists, and relatives brought hip hop gear from the United States. Many people had VCRs, so aspiring hip hoppers could see prerecorded video clips. And they could listen to Miami radio station 99 Jamz FM.

Soon after I returned to Cuba for the third time in May 2001, I sat out on the balcony of the *casa particular* in Vedado with

Magia and Alexey. Alexey related that, when he was growing up in the eighties, he was attracted by the energy and soulfulness of the rap music that came along the airwaves of 99 Jamz FM. As a kid he would build antennas from wire coat hangers and dangle his radio out the window, "crazy to get the 99." On episodes of *Soul Train* beamed in from Miami television, Alexey saw b-boying for the first time. He copied the steps and then showed them to the kids in the neighborhood. Alexey remembered the dance cyphers in the park El Quijote. Kids would form a circle. In the center the b-boys would polish the concrete with their back spins and windmills, while others broke into a beatbox or rhymed.

Alexey liked to work with his hands, whittling pieces of wood into elaborate statues and religious objects. He was working as a sculptor when he met Magia and they decided to get married. Magia shared a one-bedroom apartment on Calle Jovellar in Central Havana with her mother and sister. She moved in with Alexey's family, which had a small rooftop terrace apartment in the industrial suburb of Regla.

At this time Alexey was writing lyrics and rhyming in a rap group with two other guys. But the other two stopped coming to rehearsals, and Alexey was writing and rehearsing by himself. Eventually, he asked Magia if she would form a group with him. Magia initially joined the group as a way of supporting her husband and creating a space outside the daily routine of married life that wasn't just about cooking, cleaning, home, and work. "I began with the group just singing the chorus," Magia said. "But later Alexey began to give me room so that I could rap about issues relating to women. Eventually, I earned my position within the group as a rapper. To be honest, I never thought I'd ever leave the bedroom and perform in front of an audience. I'm actually a very shy person, but I've overcome that bit by bit."

Magia and Alexey, like other Cubans of the hip hop generation, had little or no memory of the early years of the revolution. They'd heard stories from their parents about the literacy campaign that mobilized 1.25 million Cubans or about the deseg-regation of whites-only spaces during the 1960s. As the younger

© Oriana Eliçabe

Magia López and Alexey Rodríguez of Obsesión

generation, they had benefited from the extension of education, housing, and health care to black families. But they came of age during the Special Period, as the revolutionary years gave way to times of austerity, and racism was visible once again.

In a society where it was taboo to talk about race publicly, racism was the elephant in the room. Fidel had attempted to create a color-blind society, where equality between blacks and whites would make racial identifications obsolete. But in redrawing the geography of Cuba's racial landscape, the state simultaneously closed down Afro-Cuban clubs and the black press. As racism became public once again during the Special Period—it had never really gone away—blacks were left without the means to talk about it. When called on their racism, officials trotted out the same tired line—*en Cuba, no hay racismo* (in Cuba, there is no racism). My trusty manual, *The Cuban Revolution and Its Extension*, had referred to racial prejudice in Cuba as "no more than a disappearing legacy of the past." But I saw how my black friends were harassed by police and asked for ID. I saw that they had a harder time getting jobs in tourism than their white peers.

© Yoel Diaz Vazquez

Alexey Rodríguez

It was at this juncture that hip hop culture appeared and took root. While the black nationalism espoused by an earlier generation of visiting black radicals like Marcus Garvey or Stokely Carmichael never had much appeal in Cuba, African American rappers spoke a language of black militancy that resonated with Cuban youth. It spoke to their experiences of racial discrimination in the Special Period. Young Cubans of African ancestry proudly referred to themselves as black.

"I am what my image shows, a black woman," declared Magia, in her rap "Niche niche," the Cuban slang for dark skinned. "Representing those women who dare to get out there / My skin is the color of night, it reveals secrets already known / To show that which is hidden is seen by all."

Cuban rap was bold and rebellious. But, after all, isn't that what you would expect from a generation of young people raised under a revolutionary government? The daily youth periodical was called *Juventud Rebelde* (Rebellious Youth). In daycare centers and schools, children repeated the motto "We will be like Che." We're talking about a place where the evening news called for resistance to US imperialism and global capitalism. But, with Cuban rap, it was different. It was different because the children of the revolution were turning the tables on the establishment revolutionaries. The younger people were taking the slogans and analysis they were taught and were using them to question the changes going on around them. If the birthright of the revolution was to make all Cubans equal, they asked, why were some more equal than others? Why were blacks not treated the same as whites?

Magia was part of a new breed of emcees, agnostic and irreverent, the voices of an urban culture that was—as the chorus to her song went—made in Havana City. But she didn't see herself as a dissident. Although she never was affiliated with the Communist Youth League, Magia had a strong sense of identification with the revolution. She often found herself defending the government in conversations with her more skeptical peers. I wondered how it was possible to be both a fierce critic of race relations and a defender of the revolution. Wouldn't there come a point where you would have to choose sides?

The question of being original is not *pretending* to be original. It's simply to *be original*." Alexey's voice swooped climactically on the last two words in his usual theatrical style. Obsesión was performing on stage at Cubadisco, the annual music contest sponsored by the Cuban music industry and held in the beachside district of Playa. Waves were crashing in the background on that late spring evening as floodlights lit the makeshift stage. Alexey wore his hair in short locks, a beaded black-and-yellow chain around his neck. On the front of his t-shirt was the image of the African American journalist and death-row prisoner Mumia Abu Jamal.

"Is it true or not?" Alexey, aka El Tipo Este, asked as he primed the audience of mostly young black Cubans in baseball caps, Fila sweatshirts, and basketball jerseys. The clothing styles, like the handshakes and the American slang that peppered their speech, highlighted their identity as young black Cubans. There was a sprinkling of *noviacitas*, young foreign women brought by their Cuban boyfriends. "This is the story that emcees have to take from the *loco, loco*, El Tipo Este, baptized today, the commentary begins." The booming beat sounded four or five times in quick succession, and then the rhythm kicked in.

"Every person / In my barrio / Every person / In my barrio," Magia repeated the refrain to the song, over and over. She was wearing a red-and-white paisley head wrap with an African gown, large hoop earrings, and a necklace made of small cowry shells. It brought to mind Afrocentric American rappers like Yo-Yo, Harmony, and Isis.

Magia began a rap-skit with El Tipo Este. "I was thinking of finding myself a foreigner / One that has a lot of money."

"Of course," El Tipo Este interjected.

"I don't care what he's like / I just want someone who'll resolve my problems. It's a sacrifice but you get results / Love in these times that we live is relative / I'm a young woman who has to secure her future, you get me? / I'm not the kind to look for work or nothin' / I want to travel, and help my family from abroad / My wedding has to be beautiful, like in the Hollywood movies."

"Run for the city, a commentary," they both chanted on the chorus. "Is it a *jinetera*, a bunch of crazies doing tourism, tell me where, chico?"

"I was thinking that an intellectual such as myself," El Tipo Este rapped in a pompous tone.

"Like you?" asked Magia.

"Shouldn't be wasting time with these people / Who don't have a sufficient cultural level / To have a conversation that matches my social position / I don't support this language everyone is using / '*Asere*,' '*¿qué bolá?*' You find it all over the place / you know, with these people of the *solares*."

"Yo, yo, yo, I was thinking," she replied: "All the hours I've studied haven't served for nothin' / Whole mornings studying / I'm going to leave my career, papa / I'm very sorry, I won't be an engineer / My girl just called, there's a job in tourism / Tourism, papa / It's cleaning floors, but who cares? / It'll give me a few bucks and I can resolve some problems."

"I was thinking, why don't I / Form a combo and start performing traditional music?" rapped El Tipo Este. "I'll be part of the *farándula* [new elite] / I'll play Son de la Loma, and Chan Chan."

"And Guantanamera," added Magia.

The song alluded to the contradictions of Havana in the 1990s. Education was no longer a ticket to social mobility. Professional occupations were less remunerative than hustling or performing traditional Cuban songs for tourists. Obsesión was critical of this reality. As the audience laughed and clapped, I sized the people up. Some of the young Cuban men there with foreign girlfriends were *jineteros*. Wasn't that a contradiction, I wondered, being at an underground rap concert and at the same time wanting the nice things and trips around the city that came from befriending foreigners? Couldn't they see that the Obsesión song was actually a parody of the *jinetero* lifestyle, a criticism of the "easy fix" as a way to acquire material possessions and move up in the world?

The next group on stage, Explosión Suprema, had a notice-ably different energy. Miki Flow wore a t-shirt that read "USA." Brebaje Man was his co-rapper.

"Where are my people from Alamar?" Miki Flow called out. "We come from out in the sticks, man, from Alamar." Alamar was a district on the periphery of Havana that contained a series of low-income housing projects. Miki Flow switched into hip hop Spanglish, a combo of American and Cuban slang. "¿Qué bolá, asere? Wasssssup? Aqui, en Cubadisco, manos pa' arriba, Explosión Suprema in da house."

"Aiiiight. Represent the real hi ho," added Brebaje Man, trun-cating his sentences Cuban style. "Manos pa' arriba. No doubt. Yo, check it out, check it out."

Bouncing across the stage, Miki Flow began his song "Mi patria, caray!" (My country, damn!). As a rapper, he said, he represented the essence of Cubanía: "Although my lyrics are not mixed with *son* / Everything that I'm singing here is very Cuban."

"Undergroun', almost without possibilities," rapped Brebaje Man.

"But with the little that we have we ain't *gusanos* [maggots]," he continued, using the derogatory label often given to people who had renounced the revolutionary government.

"I'm like a magician on the stage," Miki Flow went on. "Raising a dead public till they laugh with happiness / Making disappear their agony and their sadness."

"Shuttup, shuttup New York / Shuttup, shuttup, mothafuka," they rapped, concluding the song. Miki Flow and Brebaje Man gesticulated and grimaced as they threw in the English expletives "fuck you" and "mothafuka." It struck me that this in-your-face pose was what resonated with local youth across language barri-ers. When Cubans heard American music, they didn't understand the lyrics for the most part. They didn't speak English. But there was something about the *attitude* of American rappers that spoke to them, that communicated all the frustration and pent-up anger of a life lived on the margins. I wondered what it was about Alamar that could produce such burning music.

Brebaje Man

© Yoel Diaz Vazquez

Following Explosión Suprema, Randy came up onto the stage. Gone was the skinny adolescent who had rapped with his baby cousin about his bicycle. Randy was now a tall, broad-shouldered young man, his hair braided in cornrows. Randy had joined with Jesse Saldrigas, aka El Huevo, and with another rapper they formed the group Los Paisanos. The group had lost the other rapper, who had decided to switch to a commercial genre of salsa-rap fusion and signed a record deal with a foreign label. In a song called "El barco" (The boat), Randy rapped about the life of an underground rapper:

My form of dress means that in the street
They ask for my ID, despite the fact that when I was a kid
I also cried, "We will be like Che."
Now I'm found seated on the bench of the accused,
Not with crossed arms, but there's no *fokin* place in the market
For people like me, who haven't taken on the word mixture or
    fusion.
If rap is rap and tango is tango,
Then why do we make this "rice with mango."

"We're a boat that's adrift, in the middle of a storm," they rapped on the chorus. "We're a boat that's adrift, and the captain is called rap / We're a boat that's adrift, that navigates without direction / And with no money we've lost half the crew." Cuban rap was penniless and adrift. And so was Randy, trying to navigate his way around sweet-talking label reps and defend himself against cops. He had outgrown his bicycle and was now forced to fend for himself in a boat that was lost at sea.

One of the last acts of the night, the group Hermanos de Causa, came onto the stage. "Buenas noches, Playa," said Soandry, serious and without the hype of the previous performers. "We're Hermanos de Causa. We're from the barrio, from Alamar." A synthesized beat, overlaid with conga, entered the background. After a four-bar interlude a drum sample brought the rhythm, and Soandry began to rap:

> I have a race that is dark and discriminated
> I have a work day that demands and gives nothing
> I have so many things that I can't even touch them
> I have facilities I can't even step foot in
> I have liberty between parentheses of iron
> I have so many benefits without rights that I'm imprisoned
> I have so many things without having what I had

The tone was understated, quiet yet damning. It was this generation's answer to the Afro-Cuban poet Nicolás Guillen, who in his 1964 poem "Tengo" (I have) had praised the achievements of the revolution for Afro-Cubans: "I have, let's see, that I have learned to read, to count. I have that I have learned to write and to think." There was a striking contrast between the imaginative ideal of the revolution—the one that I had also come to Cuba seeking—and the new realities of hardship and shortage. Young black Cubans were part of a generation who were promised a utopia, and reality fell far short.

From problems of transportation to *jineterismo*, racial inequality, police harassment, and the lure of foreign labels, the global art form of rap was speaking directly to very local issues.

© Jason Florio

Hermanos de Causa

But could this localness and directness also make rappers too visible and vulnerable to censorship? After all, Cuban artists had perfected techniques of metaphor, allusion, and ambiguity. Filmmakers like the legendary "Titon," as the late Tomás Gutiérrez Alea was known, or the black director Sergio Giral, had always chosen historical themes like slavery as a way to comment on race. Similarly, sometimes the trick for rappers was making a local theme seem not very local at all.

Magia had written a song, "La llaman puta" (They call her whore), and she asked me to do the vocals on it. Over several weeks in June we rehearsed the song for an upcoming concert featuring Obsesión at the Cine Riviera. The concert was to be a prelude to the annual rap festival held out at Alamar. A few days before the event, we did a final run-through of the show in the apartment that Magia and Alexey shared with his parents in the small peninsula town of Regla.

In lieu of a prerecorded beat for her song, Magia decided to bring in Banderas, a student of slight build from the Instituto Superior, to play percussion. Banderas opened up, keeping time with the shaking of a caxixi, a woven basket rattle. Someone else picked up a cowbell known as a *campana* and struck it on the last two beats of the bar. "They call her *puta* / For most that's not more than a slut, making use of / The fact of her beauty." Magia began her rap over the sparse instrumentation.

Banderas passed on the caxixi to someone else and switched to the batá. The three instruments together created a deep polyrhythmic pulse. The pace of Magia's rap quickened, evoking a sense of frenzy. "Crazy / Flesh that invites, that excites, provokes ..."

"She hurries the movements of her hips because outside waits another client," Magia continued the rap. "It could be a drunk, it could be a lunatic / An elegant type, or an assassin / Who comes hidden in a masculine body / How many go down this path, and then they call her *puta*."

I sang the chorus, a Yoruba chant: "Maripu yeye, eruwe, eruwe, eruwe. Maripu yeye, Amala, amala, amala." "Yelode," cried Magia at the end of each phrase. She rapped,

They call her whore, society rejects her
Prostitute: she who sells herself for money is not discussed
Every day the same thing, with the fear gathered between her
    legs
Every man is a test of her love for her family
Every man distances her more from men
Men, two points of shit!
This is the conclusion of her life …
Imagine that everyone turns against you, woman
There's no money
It's not that the little you have doesn't stretch
It's that you're broke
You're outta luck, but this time more than usual
Your head is splitting, looking for solutions
The father of your child, don't even mention him
You're scrambling around for any work you can find,
Desperate, but the game is tight
You go once and a million times, but nothing
Even in your dreams you hear the sound of doors slamming in
    your face.

All of us, including me, had heard the song countless times yet were struck by the darkness of the lyrics. This was no light-hearted skit like "Run for the City."

"Coñyyoooo," Alexey exhaled. We all sat silently.

"Do you think things are so bad as that here?" I asked Magia.

"Well, you know, I'm not talking about Cuba in the song," she responded, a little defensively. "I'm talking about capitalist societies, where women are forced into prostitution. The *jineteras* here just want pretty things, makeup, a new television set."

"I don't agree with that, chica," said Yelandy, the manager of Obsesión. "It's true that the revolution takes care of us all, but things have changed. It's not so easy to make your paycheck cover your expenses."

"But I can see Magia's point," I chimed in. "In the United States, the majority of people don't have adequate health coverage and housing. And education, which you need to get a decent job, is more the privilege of an elite than a right. At least here Cubans have their basic needs taken care of by the government." I could hear the preachiness in my voice, could sense the others tuning out, thinking, *We've only heard this a million times before.* But I went on with my lecture. "Most of the *jineteros* that I see seem to be after foreigners to have a good time or to get nice stuff."

"That's not true," responded Yelandy. "Not everybody is doing it to get a new Gucci handbag or a video player from Carlos Tercera. Some people do it to support their families and to meet their basic necessities."

"Well, what about people who aren't doing it to support their families?" I responded. "Some people have enough breadwinners in their family to cover all their basic expenses, but they only go after foreigners. They want to go to the fancy clubs and on vacations and have nice things. That's not about necessity."

"Maybe it's not about necessity for certain people," Yelandy conceded. "But sometimes we want to have choices. Most of us have to live with our parents, even after we get married and have kids of our own. We do the same old job, day in and day out, and that's not even to earn enough to go on a vacation or buy a computer. In your country you can move away from home and rent an apartment, and you can earn money and travel around the world. Why shouldn't Cubans have the right to do that, too? Doesn't everyone want a different life, to have adventures?"

Yelandy was right. I imagined myself back in the same house in Sydney where I had grown up, twenty-seven years old, living with my parents, still waitressing at Barbara's Bar and Café. I saw myself making café lattes for the rest of my life, and I shuddered at the thought.

"I'm not saying that things are easy." Magia broke my reverie. "But still, I don't want people to get the wrong impression. The manager of the Cine Riviera is already worried about some of our other songs that are not even so *fuerte* as this one. You have to understand, it was tough even convincing him to let us do a rap concert in his theater."

It struck me that Magia did intend the song to have a local resonance. She was claiming that it was a song about capitalist countries. But Magia had never seen a capitalist country. She had never even left Cuba. Just as Titon and Giral had defended their films by saying that they took place in a prerevolutionary past, so Magia was preparing her defense. And this defense would allow her to use the platform of the high-profile Cine Riviera to provoke conversations about a reality that she did know very well—that of the poor black women who worked the streets in neighborhoods like Central Havana, where she had grown up.

So what was *I* defending?

Rap music may have carried a negative stigma with theater managers and event promoters, but *salseros* were the centerpiece of Cuba's emerging tourist culture. A few weeks later I went with Randy's mother, Lily, to an afternoon show at the Casa de la Música (House of Music) in Miramar. The neighborhood had been upscale in prerevolutionary times but was now populated by tourist hotels and the small-scale mansions of foreign embassies; the elegant former homes of upper-class exiles were occupied by multiple working-class Cuban families. The Casa de la Música used to be a popular venue for local Cubans, who would go there on weekends to dance, drink rum, and listen to salsa. It used to cost five pesos for an afternoon show and ten pesos for an evening show. But by the 1990s the Casa de la Música could no longer finance its operations. It began charging forty pesos for afternoon shows and ten dollars at night. With an afternoon show costing more than half their weekly salary, Cubans stopped coming to shows. It was now tourists, accompanied by *jineteros*, who danced, drank rum, and enjoyed the salsa bands.

The cabaret-like atmosphere of the Casa de la Música, with its dimmed lights, round tables with white tablecloths, and neatly attired waiters, contrasted with the bright Caribbean midafternoon sunlight outside. As Lily and I entered the place, we squinted as our eyes slowly adjusted to the darkness. The tableau that materialized before us was strangely reminiscent of a Batista-era nightclub, except that the North American steamship owners and businessmen had been replaced by Canadian joint venture executives, pink-faced German tourists, and aging British matrons. A Cuban woman in a tight fluorescent-pink dress fawned over an obese white man in a flower print shirt to our left. In front of us two Cuban youths in guayabera shirts competed with each other for the attention of a tourist.

The feature band for the afternoon was Dan Den, a salsa dance band founded by Juan Carlos Alfonso. After a few upbeat dance numbers Dan Den switched into the song "Atrevido" (Daring) by the Spanish-based Cuban rap group Orishas. The rap song was about a couple who move from the provinces to Havana and swindle tourists as a way of bringing themselves out of rural poverty.

The lead singer of Dan Den chanted from the chorus to the Orishas' song: "Everything that she asked for."

The Cubans in the audience shouted back, "El punto se la gastaba!" (The idiot paid out.)

"A pretty room in the Cohiba," the singer intoned.

"The idiot paid out!"

"A dress for her, and a shirt for me."

"The idiot paid out!"

"If she wanted to go to the beach."

"The idiot paid out!"

"He was running out of money, but …"

"The idiot paid out!"

"To dance at a concert with Orishas."

"The idiot paid out!"

The call-and-response went on for the whole chorus. The Cubans were dancing and singing along, especially the *jineteros* who were there with foreigners. They punctuated their line with emphatic glee, all the while smiling and flirting with their foreigners, who were blissfully unaware of what was going on—even if they spoke Spanish, most of the gringos couldn't understand the context or the slang of the song.

Maybe Yelandy was right about *jineterismo*'s being a source of empowerment rather than the selling of sex for consumer items. Wasn't this what the Cuban state itself was doing, *jineteando* on a global market, financing itself by selling images of white sandy beaches and decaying colonial houses to tourists? Perhaps this was what the ideal of revolution had become—just another Che Guevara ashtray or t-shirt peddled to those of us who came looking for it. Or was there some way that rappers could rework the vision of revolution to advance their own agenda?

As I danced along to the song that day in the Casa de la Música, I was in on the joke. I smiled smugly to myself that these other foreigners were truly being ridiculed and taken for a ride. But when I turned to share a knowing smile with Lily, I saw that she was also singing along loudly to the song, clapping her hands, and letting out whoops of joy. Hold on—what did that make me? *"The idiot paid out!"* I panicked momentarily as I mentally calculated the bus fares, price of entry, drinks. As I had rationalized, an outing with a Cuban friend meant that you offered to pay for everything. That was the only way you could be out together. And most of the time my friends insisted on paying for at least one drink—as Lily also had this afternoon—so that they didn't feel like this was a lopsided affair. But I couldn't shake the feeling that I was no different than these other foreigners, all projecting our fantasies onto Cuba and secretly being laughed at.

About six miles east of Havana, just beyond the aquamarine blue of the Caribbean Sea and the low-density shrubs of the flat plains, stand the tall rectangular buildings of the Alamar housing projects. The cement constructions are covered in chalky white paint that is peeling and eaten away in patches by the salty ocean air. Some individual blocks are painted in pink, murky green, or faded red. Here and there is a palm tree or a children's swing set. Apartments are connected by sets of diagonal stairways that begin from the ground up. The design is angular and solid. It is no-frills, functional proletarian housing. On the tops of the buildings spidery homemade antennas reach for the sky.

The five- and six-story buildings were designed by Soviet architects and built by microbrigades, or ordinary people organized into work teams, as a solution to housing shortages in Havana in the 1970s. Slum clearance programs relocated black

© Jason Florio

Alamar

communities to Alamar from shantytowns such as Llega y Pon, Las Yaguas, and Palo Cagao. The 1970s were a grim era of Cuban history, known euphemistically as the *quinquenio gris* (gray five years—that actually lasted closer to fifteen years), when the orthodoxy of Soviet socialism overshadowed cultural and social life on the island. The heavy and somber buildings—nicknamed "Siberia" by their residents—immortalized the essence of those years. With a population of 300,000 in more than two thousand buildings, Alamar is the largest housing project in the world. Each prefabricated building bears a stenciled number—D 42, Zona 2—the impersonal stamp of the assembly line.

If Havana was hard hit by the crisis of the Special Period, Alamar was even more so. The gasoline shortages meant transportation into the city was less frequently available, and there were longer waits, making it difficult for people to get to work. There were no tourists around to hustle dollars from. And the contained nature of the apartments made it harder for residents to start up small businesses—like the bodegas cropping up around Central Havana—with people selling ice cream, pastries, or pizza from the front windows of their homes. There were frequent blackouts, water problems, and shortages of cooking gas. And for the young people of the projects, there was nothing to do. It's no wonder that Alamar, often compared with the South Bronx, has been seen as the capital of rap in Cuba.

Havana was fast becoming a tourist mecca. But I imagined that Alamar might be the source of a more potent and revolutionary hip hop culture, because its rappers were not tempted by the lure of record deals or subject to the watchful eye of cultural officials. It was here in Alamar that American rappers were brought by the Black August Hip Hop Project to perform before large crowds of Cuban youth at the annual state-sponsored hip hop festival. What brought American rappers to this place— other than tours organized by the Communist Youth League? Could they reach out to Cuban youth with their language of black power? And why would the Cuban state sponsor this gathering of revolutionary black artists? Citing the "divisive effects" of race-based politics, Cuban officials had long been suspicious of visiting black nationalists, with their dashikis and Afros.

In late June I decided to visit Alamar for a prefestival rap concert at the Alamar amphitheater. To get there I had to take a bus that left from the stop at 29 and the Avenida de los Presidentes, a few blocks from where I was staying in El Vedado. As I approached the bus stop, I saw long lines of people just waiting—a familiar enough sight in Cuba; they were spread out along the walls and clumped under the shade of citrus trees.

"¿El ultimo?" I called out as I walked to the end of the waiting masses, per the convention at all places where Cubans queued for services—train stations, fish shops, *panaderias*, government offices, and the famous state-run ice cream parlor, Coppelia. "Who is last?" A young woman in a green lycra tank top and striped leggings signaled me. "OK, I'm behind you," I told her, and she nodded listlessly.

After about twenty minutes a *camello* bus wheezed its way to the stop, belching black smoke and diesel fumes. *Camellos* were bulky pink steel vehicles dubbed camels because of their humps in the back and front. They were constructed out of eighteen-wheeler semis and were yet another solution to the transportation crisis. Instead of all rushing for the bus, the waiting people recalled who they were behind and entered the bus in an orderly fashion. In this way another two buses filled up, and finally—about one hundred people and two hours later—I paid my twenty centavos and was on my way to Alamar.

At the concert in Alamar I met Julio Cardenas, aka El Hip-Hop Kid. He was a tall guy with a short afro and an earnest expression. Julio was raised by his mother in the neighboring sector of Guanabacoa. As a kid he would come rushing home from school to watch the b-boys *retandose* and *retarse*—battling—and *tirando cartones*, laying out the cardboard strip, on the back patio of his building. He and his friends watched *Beat Street*, *Fast Forward*, and *Breakin'* and copied the moves. Julio moved to Alamar when he was fifteen, and he became caught up in the hip hop movement that was taking Alamar by storm. He would go to the *moños*, or block parties, where people rapped and deejayed.

After Julio finished school, he went on to technical college to do a degree in civil construction. But he graduated at the height of the Special Period, when there were no jobs. So he went to work with his grandfather in a nearby fishery, for some cash to help out his mother and to get the local authorities off his back. Eventually, he found a job as a bridge operator, raising and lowering the bridge that connected Alamar and Cojimar, to allow the ships to pass through. The job was a no-brainer. At 7 a.m. Julio would raise the bridge. By early afternoon, when all the boats had gone through, he would sit back with his friends and exchange news about who had the latest rap magazine from the States, whether they'd heard this song from The Pharcyde or EPMD.

In 1996 Julio formed the group Raperos Crazy de Alamar (RCA) with Carlito "Melito," a carpenter, and Yoan. They started out just to amuse themselves, without ambitions of being serious artists. "That moment we were living was so critical, so boring," related Julio. "Everything was closed off and censured. We, the youth, were doing hip hop just to do something, looking for a way of having fun."

I was reminded of the young people I knew back in Sydney who had also looked to hip hop as a way out of the boredom. It wasn't the same boredom of kids in the suburbs who wanted reprieve from their sheltered existence. It was the boredom of low-paying menial jobs and truncated opportunities. The rap scholar Tricia Rose identified this need to break the cycle of boredom and alienation as one of the factors that underlay the rise of hip hop in its birthplace, the Bronx.[2] While Cuba presented quite specific conditions of economic crisis, combined with political restrictions, I realized that this void wasn't something peculiar to Cuba. And hip hop wasn't just a distraction from the void. It was a way of re-creating a sense of community and finding spaces of pleasure in the face of atomization, isolation, and the regimentation of life.

Julio and his friends listened to American rap, but they didn't understand the lyrics, and they had no clue how to write their own songs. One day Julio was at Pablo's house listening to his latest CDs. He heard the song "Boricuas on Da Set," by Fat Joe, featured on a compilation album. Hearing the song was a turning point in his life. "'Coñyyyyoooo,'ta buena,' I said, when I heard it," Julio related. "It was a moment that touched my heart and opened my mind. I was hearing a lot of music from Miami radio, LL Cool J, 2 Live Crew, Queen Latifah, Monie Love, but that song inspired me. I thought it could really be the Latino-American-Cuban connection."

Pablo copied Fat Joe's song for Julio on a cassette. Julio would listen to the poor-quality recording on his old beat-up Walkman over and over, every day. "I liked the beat, but I didn't know what to do," said Julio. "I didn't know anything about flow, cadence, rhythm. I'd never studied music. Wow! How am I gonna do it? At the start it was all a joke. But every day I began to think about a vision of how I wanted to do the song. What was guiding me was the sound of the voices, the mixture of each, and the cadences. I started to rap over the top of this song, write my first lyrics. So when Fat Joe said, 'Oh Boricuas, clap your hands,' I started saying, 'Todo el mundo con los manos arriba, negros, mulattos, blancos.' That was the basis of my first rap, 'Hip Hop Es Mi Cultura.' It was an old-school rap, but it reached the people."

RCA tried out at the hip hop festival auditions later that year. The musicians faced a panel of three judges—a professor of visual arts, a professor of drama, and a poet who said that their lyrics were undeveloped, lacking in content, and violent. Julio was incensed. "*Asere*, you don't know shit about rap," he thought to himself. "You've never listened to rap in your life! How you gonna sit there and tell me what is rap?"

But by 1999 RCA had not only passed the auditions—they were the stars of a festival that had included the famous African American artists Mos Def, Talib Kweli, DJ Hi-Tek, dead prez, and Common. The encounter was anticipated with much emotion and excitement by the Cubans. When dead prez rapped, "I'm an African, I'm an African," in front of a crowd of thousands at the festival, the amphitheater resounded with the thundering response of the Cuban audience chanting back the words. It was

Pan-Africanism in motion. But the politics didn't always translate. Unaware of the implications of what he was about to do, the rapper M-1 pulled out a dollar bill on stage and began to burn it with a cigarette lighter, an act considered illegal and a defacement of property in the United States. "Because of this dollar, the children in my country are dying for crack or for drugs or for bling bling." The audience went wild. How could he be burning a precious dollar bill? "Oye, no, gimme that dollar, I can buy some bread, or some french fries," people in the audience cried out. Then he began to burn a ten-dollar bill. "Nooooo! Stop!" screamed the audience. "What is that crazy fucker doing? I could feed my whole family for a month with that." One member of the American delegation, Raquel Rivera, was translating, explaining to the baffled audience that in America black people are dying because of the dollar bill. "But here in Cuba," shouted one person, half-seriously, "people are dying of hunger."

Then, inexplicably, during the performance of the pioneer American rapper Mos Def, people started leaving the stadium. "Reyes de la Calle are better than Mos Def," said some kids on their way out. "We can't understand anything he says."

The Latino-American-Cuban connection was somewhat tenuous when subjected to the very real differences of language, culture, and history. First, Alamar was not the South Bronx. Black Cuban youth did have access to higher education—Julio had finished his degree in civil construction—even if that education didn't necessarily lead to jobs. They did not live in communities ravaged by crack or other drugs, and bling bling was a remote concept, given Cuba's endemic scarcities.

Second, the black militancy of the American rappers was not comparable to the racial consciousness of Cuban rappers. Black Cuban identity—always expressed within the boundaries of an anticolonial nationalism—was not equivalent to American blackness, shaped through the fiery battles about slavery, desegregation, and civil rights. Cubans didn't have a civil rights movement that brought a discussion of race out into the open. The black-white dichotomy of American race relations did not exist in Cuba. While in much of America even "one drop" of black blood socially categorized a person as black, Cubans had a much broader spectrum of racial classifications—from the darker-skinned *prietos, morenos,* and *negros* to the mixed-race *pardos* and *mulatos.* The militant stance of American rappers, particularly their language of racial justice, appealed to the Cubans. But the categories of American racial politics established by Jim Crow laws in the early twentieth century could not be superimposed on a culture in which racial identity was not so clearly spelled out.

Like me, the Black August rappers had come seeking to make connections with Cuban rappers as part of the hip hop universe. But the possibility of marginalized people around the world uniting in a hip hop fellowship was starting to seem increasingly like fantasy; the black planet was more the wishful thinking of a handful of intellectuals and socially conscious rappers than a reality. Were we guilty of what the hip hop scholar Imani Perry has called a "romantic Afro-Atlanticism" that ignores the deeply conflicted interactions between people of African descent in the "New World"?[3] The idea of a shared aesthetic culture that travels between diasporic communities didn't take into account the deep residues that national belonging left behind.

As the century drew to a close, American rap was no longer the epicenter of hip hop for Cubans. Cuban rap was starting to take on its own voice, to develop its own stars and pioneers. RCA closed the 1999 festival, receiving as much applause, if not more, than the American artists. "This was a defining moment for us as a movement," recalled Julio. "Despite the fact that they were rappers from the US, from the mecca of the world—New York— they weren't better than us. We were rapping and expressing our own realities to our own people."

The annual hip hop festival in Alamar was started in June 1995 by an association of rappers known as Grupo Uno. The rappers worked on a shoestring budget to make the concerts happen, sometimes without electricity, dependent on an ailing sound system or resources donated by friends and neighbors. By the time of the 1999 festival, the Cuban state had become more involved. It provided a professional sound system, transportation to and from the events, and even food for rehearsals. And after the 2000 festival, the state disbanded Grupo Uno and entrusted the Youth League with the organization of the festivals. The absorption of hip hop into the state was underway.

At the same time the state itself was evolving in response to pressures from citizens. The appointment of the long-haired poet Abel Prieto as minister of culture was a reflection of the changes taking place in the cultural sphere. In July 2001 Prieto met with rappers to talk about forming a rap agency. After the meeting he pledged his support to Cuban rap as a movement that profoundly reflects "the theme of racial discrimination" and "highlights the dramas of marginalized barrios." It was the first time an official had talked publicly about race and marginality. And with this newfound legitimacy, rappers began to play more of a role in organizing their festival. Rather than having music professors sitting as judges on the panels, by the 2001 festival it was the rappers themselves who were adjudicating.

"I represent my ancestors, my African roots," rapped a white Cuban guy with light brown hair.[4] He formed the group Los Padrinos with a black Cuban guy. They were trying out at the hip hop festival auditions. I looked over at the panel of five judges: Magia, Alexey, Pablo, Ariel, and Yosmel, a rapper from the group Anónimo Consejo. But there was not even the shadow of a smirk on their faces. Either they were maintaining a professional demeanor in keeping with their task, or, more likely, they were unfazed by a white rapper's paying homage to his African ancestry. Cuban national identity was promoted by postindependence intellectuals as a composite of African and Spanish cultures. It was not seen as odd for a white rapper to claim his African roots because these were the shared roots of the nation and not only of black Cubans.

"Gracias." Magia nodded at the duo when they finished their audition. Then each judge turned to jot down notes on a piece of paper with three categories: flow, lyrics, and projection. These were the criteria that were being used to judge the rappers. Magia had explained to me earlier that of the two hundred or so groups trying out in auditions across the country, seventeen would be selected from Havana and three from the provinces. Seven other groups, which were officially employed in state music agencies—these included Obsesión, Instinto, and Anónimo Consejo—were also in the festival lineup, along with five foreign groups.

I spotted my friend Lily. Lily had recently found a small one-room apartment in Cotorro, a distant suburb of Havana by the main highway. Randy still spent most of his time in the barrio of Almendares, where his grandparents lived. Lily was at every one of Randy's shows and had now come to support him at his audition. She was listening and learning about the rap that he was so passionate about.

Randy and El Huevo were up next. After being rejected during the 2000 festival auditions, Randy had gone away and worked hard at his craft, practicing every day. He sauntered onto the stage, winking at his mother. He was confident. He was lyrically in good shape. His friends were now on the panel of judges. They knew his skills. I crossed my fingers for him.

"Nearly all of my friends in jail / My barrio full of the mothers left behind," he rapped. "Some jump into the sea, others go crazy, commit suicide / Death is a phase of life / I look for an exit and I don't find it / I'm at the center of a pack of hungry wolves / In the bullshit of the streets." Then they chanted on the chorus, "What will be, what will be, what will be / What will be of my life? What will be?"

"I study, she works, I hardly see my mother," Randy continued his rap. "I'm missing my father, I don't know what will happen / For the last five years I'm the man of the house / Those who know me accept me and those who don't reject me / Because the streets have become my second home."

At the end of their performance, the small crowd erupted into claps and cheers. His rap had spoken of the dramas of the marginalized barrios that the minister was talking about. But for the festival Randy and El Huevo's rap would have to be more sanitized than this. I looked over at the blank faces of the judges and felt a pang for Randy. This was not the positive and educational rap that I felt Magia was probably looking for. But maybe there was a still a chance.

A few auditions later the judges decided to wrap for the day. There was still another day of auditioning in Havana and then on to the provinces. Rappers anxiously waited to hear whether they had a coveted spot in the festival.

He didn't make it again." Lily's tone was bitter when she called to give me the news about Randy. "Two years in a row. Last year they were rejected, but at the festival they were called up onto the stage and people loved them. This year, well, you saw the crowd at the auditions. The crowd was really into their performance, but that doesn't count for anything."

"What happened?" I probed, my heart sinking. "What reason did they give?"

"I don't know. Randy is not in an agency. He doesn't have any connections. I know it's a form of censorship, too. His lyrics are too *fuerte*. He doesn't understand. He says to me, 'Mama, groups that are not as good as us, who don't perform as regularly as us, were accepted for the festival this year, but not us.'"

"I'm sure he'll get called on stage again this year," I reassured her. "And people will eventually see that they are really doing great work."

"I don't think so. What chance does he have of making it now? The rap festival is the ultimate recognition for your career. It's the path to getting into an agency, getting a CD contract, and actually getting paid for shows. Randy has no desire to rap anymore."

"Tell him he shouldn't be discouraged by this. It's not a comment on the quality of his skills," I reassured her. I really believed this. "He'll find a way around the official path to success. He'll find his own way." But of this I wasn't so sure. Randy already knew there wasn't much place for him in the market, since he wasn't willing to produce a danceable sound and party lyrics. But he also felt rejected by the underground, for being too underground. This was different from Julio's experiences with the panel of professors, as the judges now were peers and equals.

But if these judges wanted to hang on to their festival, they had to make sure that the groups they selected stayed within the boundaries of what was permissible.

For those who had the honor of performing in the annual hip hop festival, there was the ritual of securing the coveted backstage pass for artists or a press pass. At the Alamar amphitheater there wasn't much of a backstage to speak of—just a narrow corridor where rappers huddled before entering the stage. The entrance fee was nominal. But more than the free entry, it was the thrill of having the blue-and-white pass enclosed in a plastic case on a string around your neck. It conferred an aura of celebrity, a sense of importance and urgency, even if all you were doing was walking back and forth along the bleachers, trying to score weed or buy peanuts.

I wasn't really expecting to get a press pass for the August festival. The pass was mostly issued to foreign journalists, filmmakers, and select Cuban promoters. But after I spoke about Cuban hip hop on a panel at UNEAC a week before the festival, Tomás Fernández Robaina, a small and sprightly writer who was organizing the event, took my elbow and urged me to pick up my press pass on Friday at the Madriguera, a youth cultural center in Central Havana. Later that day I saw Ariel, who said that he had processed my pass and it would be waiting for me on Friday at 10 a.m. I felt smug in my newfound expectations of entering the ranks of plastic-bearing royalty. I should have realized that things in Cuba are never quite that easy.

The other thing I should have known is that when Cubans say 10 a.m., they never mean 10 a.m. At 9:58 a.m. exactly I was standing outside the Madriguera. The small cottage and open-air performance space at the Madriguera, formerly the residence of the independence-era general Máximo Gómez, was tucked away at the back of a wildly overgrown botanical garden. To get to the cottage from the main entrance on Carlos Tercera, you had to wrestle your way through a jungle of quietly spreading creepers, cedar pines, citrus, and majagua trees, fending off mosquitoes and other small ankle-biting critters. When I arrived at the Madriguera that day, there was not a soul in sight and not a sound besides the distant chugs and groans of the *camello* buses from Carlos Tercera.

Gradually, some kids in baseball caps and jeans began to drift in. An hour later Magia and Alexey showed up with some other rappers. They assumed positions on the benches outside, as if settling in for the long haul.

"¿Que paso?" I didn't understand what was happening. "They said 10 a.m. to pick up our passes, but it's after 11 and no one is here." As the words escaped my mouth, I realized the stupidity of them. Magia and Alexey exchanged looks of resignation.

"Suyee," sighed Magia, using the Cuban version of my nickname. "This is Cuba." It was a phrase I was to hear time and again.

By midday the Madriguera was humming with the excited chatter of rappers who were there to claim their backstage passes. I sat drumming my fingers on my canvas bag, checking my watch every five minutes, as if that would make the Youth League functionaries appear.

"Pizza, anyone?" Around 1 p.m. Alexey had gotten hungry and picked up pizzas from the street vendor across the street to nourish us as we waited. Perhaps *nourish* is too strong a word, as the pizzas were lumpy mounds of dough saturated in oil and sprinkled with a pungent rubbery cheese on top. You had to hold the pizza off to the side and drain off the rivulets of oil before attempting to eat it.

Finally, close to 2:30 p.m., Jorge and Arnaldo, two functionaries from the Youth League, sauntered in. They unlocked the cottage door. Once they had set themselves up inside, they began to call the names of rappers to come and collect their passes. One by one kids walked out with the precious plastic around their necks and grins on their faces.

As I sat outside, I strained to hear my name being called. Getting more and more impatient, I finally went into the cottage. Magia and Alexey were sitting with Arnaldo in one of the rooms.

"Look," I said to Arnaldo, "I've been waiting here since 10 a.m., I was told my pass would be available then. It's now after 3 p.m. Please, can you just give me my pass so that I can go home?"

Arnaldo checked his list. "I don't see your name," he said. "Sorry," he added, before turning back to a conversation.

"Ahem," I cleared my throat. "I don't think you understand. Tomás Robaina and Ariel Fernández both told me I would be getting a press pass, and they said I should pick it up here, today at 10 a.m."

"Well," Arnaldo repeated slowly, "your name is not on the list. There's nothing I can do."

I looked over to Magia and Alexey. "Perhaps you should ask Ariel, maybe he has the pass for you," offered Magia.

"No, he doesn't. Ariel told me to come and collect it here," I insisted. "I waited here today for over five hours. You know that, you were with me. How can they tell me after all of this that they don't have a press pass for me?"

I wasn't getting anywhere, so I decided to try another tactic. "What about an artist's backstage pass? I'll be performing with Magia and Alexey at the festival." Magia had asked me to sing backup vocals for the "La llaman puta" song.

Magia didn't say anything. Arnaldo shrugged his shoulders. My eyes burned with tears, born not only of frustration but of humiliation and a sense of betrayal. Why wouldn't Magia back me, argue my case with Arnaldo, question this ridiculous system? Rap was supposed to be antiestablishment. Around the globe rappers were speaking out against the powers-that-be. But I was starting to wonder whether Cuban rappers were so much a part of the system that they couldn't or wouldn't see its shortcomings. I hated myself for wanting the silly piece of plastic so badly.

"You make people come here and wait for hours, and then you say my name is not even on the list?" I lashed out at Arnaldo. "You know, I'm writing about all of these experiences and the way that you treat people." Bringing up my writing was a bad idea. "There are people back in America who support the Cuban revolution, but they don't know about all of this bureaucracy that people have to go through." Bringing up the *enemigo del norte* was an even worse idea. I was coming off as a self-righteous gringa, flaunting my foreigner credentials in a society where they were hardly going to win me support. I turned on my heel and walked out with a flourish, before Arnaldo could respond to my outburst.

On the way out I bumped into Jorge, who was sitting by the door. "Are you a foreigner?" he asked. "Yes," I mumbled, as if that last outburst hadn't proved it. "Then we don't have your pass," he responded. "All foreigners must pick up their passes at the ticket booth on the first day of the festival."

The amphitheater in Alamar was a large open-air stadium with rows of concrete blocks for seating and patches of grassy area. It had been the site of the annual rap festival since the beginning. On the opening night of the festival in August 2001, the space was filled to capacity, with a sea of young people in baseball caps, bandannas, baseball jerseys, berets, guayaberas, and checkered shirts. The stage was bathed in alternating red and blue flashes from a strobe light. A set of turntables was mounted on a plank of wood held up by giant steel drums. At the front of the stage speakers towered over the audience. Draped behind the stage was a large Cuban flag, the red triangle with a five-pointed white star visible above the pumping fists of the performers on stage. To the left of the Cuban flag was a graffiti piece that read ALAMAR in block letters at the top.

The ugly cement construction of the amphitheater, typical of the surrounding housing projects, came to life with the resounding thrum of the bass, the energy of the crowd with its hands in the air, and the tags of graffiti covering the walls.

At the closing event the group Reyes de la Calle performed a song about the *balseros*, the Cubans who leave for Miami in boats. The rappers had wanted to include images of the *balseros* on a screen behind them. This was not acceptable to the president of the Youth League. He told Ariel, "CNN may be filming it, and this would lend support to the counterrevolutionaries." So Ariel asked Reyes de la Calle to do the song without the images.

© Angel Javier Machado Leyva

DJ Flipper at Hip Hop Festival in Alamar, August 2001

The Cuban government could support the rap festival so long as rappers stayed within certain prescribed boundaries. But some rappers wanted to talk about more controversial themes than before. How long would they accept directives from the Youth League president? Censorship was not always the most workable strategy. In these circumstances there was nothing like a crisis from the North to unite Cubans and give new fire to the meaning of revolution.

"The United States is under military attack! They've blown up the World Trade Center! They've blown up the Pentagon! Now they're blowing up Peeeeeburgh!" the grandmother in the house where I stayed in El Vedado was shouting from the living room. I came running out of my room. We flicked between the two channels available on state TV. The images of planes crashing into buildings were unreal. None of the commentators seemed to know what was going on. And why would anyone want to blow up Pittsburgh? It was several hours later that the news came through about the hijackers of four planes who had reduced the twin towers to rubble and crashed into the side of the Pentagon and an empty field in rural Pennsylvania.

I sat before the television watching the grainy images of the towers imploding over and over again. I was unsure if this was yet another Hollywood disaster movie or if it really happened. Fidel was involved in the inauguration of a new school that evening. Ariel came over, and we watched the live broadcast from the school where Fidel addressed a packed hall of elementary school kids. Fidel was resplendent in his military fatigues and for three hours cajoled, provoked, and meditated on the events of the day before a group of ten- and eleven-year-olds. He expressed his sympathies for the American people. He offered the resources of the country to assist in treatment of the victims. And he urged caution on the part of the American government.

"Whenever there is a tragedy like this one, no matter how difficult to avoid it may be, I see no other way but to keep calm," advised Fidel. "And if at some point I am allowed to make a suggestion to an adversary who has been tough with us for many years, we would advise the leaders of the powerful empire to keep their composure, to act calmly, not to be carried away by a fit of rage or hatred and not to start hunting people down, dropping bombs just anywhere." He paused. "Put down that pencil," he reprimanded a schoolgirl in the audience. "Don't doodle. Try to pay attention while I'm talking."

The Casa de la Cultura in Central Havana at Carlos Tercera and Castillejo was an old mansion that had been converted into a culture center. In the back there was an open area where the Youth League had mounted a stage, set up with antiquated speakers and clunky microphone stands. Young people were milling around, waiting through numerous sound checks. Rappers responded with a combination of good humor and resignation to numerous nonfunctioning microphones. They winced at the piercing feedback that assaulted them from speakers placed too close together on the small stage.

This was July 2002 and I was back in Cuba. In the short space of ten months much had changed. Julio was one of the first of several rappers to leave Cuba—he had stayed on in New York after participating in the first US tour of Cuban rappers. He was sleeping in a room the size of a closet in the cold of the bitter New York winter and wondered whether he had made the right decision. He was not an athlete or a professional musician with a future in the US or even someone with family in the States to look out for him. He was poor and black, one of the stars of a movement that came up from nothing. To survive in New York he would have to put his music career on hold and bus tables like many other immigrants in this city.

The world had also changed irrevocably. Immediately after the 9/11 attacks, all US airspace was closed to passenger planes leaving Cuba. Canada-bound planes with tourists who had been in Cuba were forced to fly an extra nine hours along the coast of the US, a harbinger of what was to follow. The US declared a global war on terror, and the charges that Cuba is a terrorist nation resurfaced, with accusations that the island was harboring fugitives, selling biotechnology, and trading with the enemies of the US. Five Cuban nationals carrying out counter-terrorism work in the US were convicted in a federal court in Miami and sentenced to prison. There were stepped up efforts by US officials to find and prosecute former Black Panthers in Cuba. Assata Shakur—who was given political asylum in Cuba following her escape from jail in 1979—would soon be classified by the FBI as a "domestic terrorist" with a bounty of $1 million dollars on her head. Meanwhile, Cuban rappers were organizing events and had become bolder about saying things in public that earlier they had uttered only privately.

At the Casa de la Cultura, Yosmel stood before a microphone. His hair was in short dreads. Yosmel had changed his name to Sekou Umoja to emphasize his spiritual connections with Africa. He was speaking passionately to the gathered crowd. "You have people saying, 'You're Cuban, you're Cuban, but they're not, they're not.' Well, then, where did 'they' come from? They come from Africa. We have Afro-Cubans in Cuba, Afro-Americans in America, Afro-British in England, and if you're born in Russia with this color skin, are you gonna come to Cuba and try to say that I'm Russian?" He paused. There were laughs from the audience; the irony of that last comparison was not lost on them.

"You're separating yourself from who you are. This is who you are. When someone feels marginalized, it's never because they wanted to feel that way. If the government wants us to respect José Martí, if they say we are all human, then first they have to respect us." The crowd burst into cheers and whistles.

"No war, no blood, peace now," Yosmel, aka Sekou, said as he took the microphone and led the crowd in the chant. The words resounded in the small space.

"Afghanistan has been the first casualty of the war on terror," Sekou told the crowd. "Who will be next? Iraq? Maybe Cuba? We, as hip hop, say no to war and imperialism. Anónimo Consejo Revolución!" The crowd cheered. "Hip Hop Revolución. Put your fist in the air." More cheers and whistles. The aging sound equipment came to life with a few static groans. As the beat kicked in, Sekou and his rapping partner Kokino, aka Adeyeme, began to rap, "No more war, No more blood, no more hunger!" "No more war! No more deaths!" continued Adeyeme. "Talkin' 'bout something real, this ain't a game / Prepare yourself for what's coming / I know what it is, stay calm, I take action." I recognized the phrases from Fidel's speech on the night of 9/11. As the world was yet again being subjected to arbitrary acts of American imperial power, Fidel's words resonated with Cuban rappers.

Here, in a former mansion-turned-culture-house, technology courtesy of the Soviets, Cuban rappers were reworking the ideal of revolution to encompass the kind of changes they wanted to see as a local and global movement. The Hip Hop Revolución drew inspiration from the Cuban Revolution and from Fidel, but it was also connected to the motherland. And perhaps this imagined connection to Africa was what kept rappers somewhat outside the orbit of the state, even as they continued to collaborate with it. So maybe the black planet was not turning out to be a reality, but did that really matter? So long as rappers could invoke this mythical global collectivity, imagine themselves as part of it, it was still meaningful. Their ties with French record labels and African American rappers, even fans in San Diego and Montreal, gave Cuban rappers a level of recognition. When black American celebrities like Danny Glover and Harry

Anónimo Consejo

© Angel Javier Machado Leyva

Adeyeme Umoja of Anónimo Consejo

© Angel Javier Machado Leyva

Belafonte came to Cuba to meet with local rappers, it meant that they were somebody.

"Hip Hop Cuba with Africa!" the rapper Amehel of the group Profundo said to a serious and focused audience with its fists raised in the air. "Hip Hop Cuba with Vieques! The undergroun' protests Israeli repression of Palestinian children." There was a shout from someone in the audience: "Free Mumia Abu Jamal. *Libertad*."

The foreign news cameras were trained on Rubén Hernández, one of the top functionaries of the Youth League. Hernández was a white Cuban with a high forehead; he was slightly balding and plump and had a brisk businesslike manner. He was standing beneath an archway on the campus of the University of Havana, answering questions about the upcoming rap festival.

"What about the criticisms of Castro coming from the rappers? Is this a new dissident movement?" asked the reporter.

"No," replied Hernández, unmoved by the question. "The rap movement here in Cuba expresses a lot of the same ideas that you see Fidel addressing—protesting against the war, expressing solidarity with political prisoners in the US and our five brothers imprisoned for counterterrorism, denouncing *el imperio*. They are not *gusanos*, no, rap in Cuba is a revolutionary movement."

When Hernández had finished speaking with the reporter, I approached him myself. "Rap is a new component of Cuban culture," Hernández told me. "And right from the start, rap has had the support of the Youth League, which rappers see as the only institution or, sorry, I mean the institution that they can most organically incorporate into. These rappers are just kids with hardly any academic training in music. They have a formula that, although it has a social base, still lacks much in terms of aesthetics. The Youth League groups together the vanguard of the rap movement, helping it raise its level of artistic quality."

Magia was standing nearby. "He's sooo patronizing," I told her later, rolling my eyes. "How can a bunch of balding white bureaucrats think they can raise the artistic level of rappers?"

"Suyee," Magia sighed. "When you've lived in this country

for years, when you have to conduct your professional life here, you see that things don't work that way. The American press is a dangerous tool. They don't really care about helping us. They have their own agenda. And arguing with bureaucrats doesn't achieve anything."

Magia knew this from firsthand experience. This year the organization of the festival had been taken over completely by the Youth League. The panel of rapper-judges who organized the previous festival was kept in the dark. The Youth League decided on the locations, selected the sixteen groups to perform, scheduled them, and even designed the logo for sweatshirts. Ariel argued with Hernández and threatened to boycott the festival. But Magia could see that the younger rap groups would still want to participate. The festival would go ahead with no mention of the boycott in the state-controlled media and Cuban rap's pioneers would be slowly edged out of their own movement. Magia argued that the showdown should take place between the Youth League and the rap movement, not between the Youth League and individual rappers, because the league couldn't sideline a whole movement the way that it could sideline rap's leaders. Magia's intervention was characteristic of her firm yet self-effacing manner, which would unify the movement and catapult her to the head of the newly formed rap agency.

The showdown did take place at the festival that year, as rappers produced some of the most biting social commentary heard in years. The state retaliated by keeping coverage of the festival off the radio and television. Rappers started to question whether they had lost their hard-earned space. But maybe it was the impetus they needed to cut their apron strings to the state and move out on their own.

I approached the curved driveway of the Hotel Riviera and looked out onto the blue sea just beyond the Malecón. It was March 2004, and I had abandoned my jeans and t-shirts for neat slacks and a collared shirt, as befitting the faculty leader of a tour of fifteen undergraduates from Princeton University, where I was now a postdoctoral fellow.

I entered the air-conditioned environs of the hotel and walked past the bar where we had been offered complimentary cocktails and juice when we first arrived. I passed the front desk and was about to enter the elevator, when a security guard stopped me.

"*Permiso*, señora, but only guests of this hotel are allowed to go upstairs."

I was stunned for a minute. But then I pulled out my hotel card to show him that I was a guest at the hotel, and he let me through. Once upstairs I started to get angry. Why didn't they stop white tourists, or even white Cubans for that matter, from going upstairs? I grabbed a few things and went to wait in the lobby for Lily, who was coming to see me.

It had been nearly two years since I had been back to Cuba, and I waited anxiously in the lobby to see Lily. She arrived, dressed in her dark blue work suit and toting a small briefcase. We hugged. We had missed each other so much.

"Let's go up to the room," I told Lily. "You gotta see this place, there's a view of the Malecón and the cleaning staff makes these bouquets—"

"Ummm," Lily looked hesitant. "I don't know if that's a good idea."

But I grabbed her by the arm, and we made our way past the same security guard.

"Señora." His voice had a warning edge to it. "You can't go upstairs, only guests of the hotel are allowed upstairs."

"Didn't I just show you my card earlier?" I replied testily.

"Yes, but she is not a guest," he pointed at Lily.

"Let's go," Lily said quietly, her hand on my arm.

But I was just getting started. "Well, I don't see you stopping any white people here at this hotel," I told the guard. A blond-haired woman in a hat, and another white couple walked straight past us. "Why don't you stop them, huh? It's because they're white, isn't it?"

"Sorry, señora, but it is hotel policy not to allow any Cubans to enter the rooms."

"Well, that policy is ridiculous enough on its own," I retorted. I was getting incensed. "But we all know this is also about race,

because any of those people going in right now could be Cuban."
I gestured at the groups of white people entering the elevators.
"But you only stop black and brown people here. That's known
as racial profiling."

Lily was looking embarrassed. "Please, Suyee, let's just drop
it."

But I didn't want to drop it. I couldn't let these people get
away with it, and I couldn't see that this was just making Lily
feel worse.

"I want to speak with a manager," I demanded.

The manager was a middle-aged, smartly dressed white
Cuban woman in a suit and pink high heels. By the time she
came down, we were surrounded by three or four other security
guards. I explained the situation to her, and she asked for the
name of the guard. I pointed him out, but he refused to give his
name. Instead, he pulled out a list of guests from the hotel and
began looking for my name on the list.

"If your name is not on this list, then we will have to ask you
to leave the premises," he threatened. I looked at him incredulously.

"This is a case of racism," I told the gathered group. "My
friend here and I are being discriminated on the basis of our
skin color."

The guards and manager were outraged. "No, en Cuba no hay
racismo," they told me. In Cuba there is no racism. They repeated
that refrain, against which there was no argument because it was
the official line. The revolution had eradicated racism.

One guard, tanned and broad shouldered with a close buzz
cut, assured me, "Maybe you have experienced racism in the
United States, but that doesn't happen here in Cuba."

And then something unexpected happened. Lily started to
agree with them. "She is not from here, she's a foreigner," Lily
told them. "She will never understand how things are in this
country." It felt like a slap in the face. But I've spent years studying race relations in Cuba, I wanted to say to her. I understand
how racism functions here, I wanted to tell a black woman who
had spent her life under the revolution and was now just trying

to bury her disappointment and discomfort. Instead, I burst into tears.

Soon Lily was crying too, and we were both crying, tears of frustration and impotence and sadness. I imagined that Lily was crying as she remembered the nights that she spent here at the Hotel Riviera with her husband for only forty pesos a night after the revolution opened up Cuba's grandest hotels to the poor, a hotel that now she couldn't even enter. I imagined she was reminded of that husband, who left her as a young bride to raise their son on her own. I was crying because Lily was right. It finally dawned on me that the reason I really *didn't* get it was because—like the foreign reporter—I was ultimately an outsider who had to be convinced of the merits of the revolution. My Cuban friends were not brainwashed or passive. Rather, it was I who had failed to see the intricate ways Cubans negotiated their revolution. So much for the grand global movement I imagined I might find. I couldn't even connect with my own friend. And we were both crying with the emotion of seeing each other after so long, and having to share the moment with some buzz-cut security guards and a manager in pink high heels.

To avoid a scene the manager took our elbows and steered us toward the bar. "What would you like, *mi corazon*, order anything you want," she cajoled. "It's on the house. Please don't cry." We nodded dumbly, as she gave us her public relations spiel about how the client is important above all else, the new lingo of capitalism in which a customer is a customer—black, white, or brown. The guards stood together in a corner, throwing glances over our way, confident that they would not be reprimanded for just doing their job, just carrying out the policy of the hotel.

That evening I took my delegation of fifteen students to a rap concert at the Teatro America in Central Havana. "I am always a realist," rapped Hermanos de Causa in their song "Lágrimas negras" (Black tears). "Don't say that there's no racism where there's a racist / Always and wherever I come across it / I find prejudice in some form or other." The rap opens with a sample of the famous Cuban song "Lágrimas negras," brassy horns punctuating the sadness of an abandoned lover: "I weep without you knowing that my crying has black tears, black tears like my life." There was something cathartic about listening to the songs. Maybe it was the realization that the powerlessness of racism could be collectively transformed into something empowering.

After the concert, following rounds of joyous hugs and greetings from Magia, Alexey, Sekou, Adeyeme, Pablo, Randy, and others, the rappers left me and began circulating in the crowd, selling their CDs—five pesos for Cubans, five dollars for foreigners. Where did I fit now, after all these years—pesos or dollars, foreigner or Cuban? Neither. "For you, Suyee, free," they said and thrust CDs into my hands. But I was no longer living from a stack of depleting dollar bills saved from waiting tables. I had a real income. I must have bought about fifteen CDs in all. "La profesora Fernandes, now she thinks she's a big shot," joked the rappers, as I pulled out the dollars.

As soon as I got back to my hotel, I pulled out my Walkman and began listening to Obsesión's new album, *La Fabri-K*, a collaboration with the group Doble Filo. "Why should we wait? For who? Who's gonna do it, EGREM?" Alexey rhymed over a syncopated drum kit and deep bass, on the introduction to the album. "Independent production, listen to me / Yo, good or bad, it's ours, made with love and a few extra provisions / We're ready, the disposition of all my people / There's no manager, we ourselves are sufficient."

There was no way of operating as a rapper in Cuban society without depending to some degree on the state. Rappers had picked this up very early on. For some, like Randy, it made their lives much more difficult, while others had greater success at navigating the cultural bureaucracy. But as the government began to usurp the space that rappers had created, rappers responded with independent production. Maybe the DIY model was the key to a truly dynamic hip hop planet. This was a model that had already found a home in several American cities, including Chicago, a hub for independent and underground hip hop.

CHAPTER 2

Down and Underground in Chi-Town

The entrance to the Red Dog Club in Chicago's Wicker Park was through a set of staircases at the back of the club. Like much else hip hop in Chicago, you had to be with insiders to navigate the hidden labyrinths and tunnels to this world. It was September 1998. I had arrived just days earlier in Chi-town to start graduate school, and I was staying with my childhood friend Gautam Ramnath. I hadn't seen Gautam since we were awkward teens forced together at our parents' social gatherings, and I half-expected him to be a computer geek or an investment banker. To my happy surprise, he and his roommate, Mike Walsh, were neither geeks nor bankers; they were b-boys at heart and eager to introduce me to Chicago's hip hop scene.

The Red Dog was a mecca for House music—a bass-heavy, electronic style of dance music pioneered in Chicago that was highly popular among African American youth. But this Saturday night the club was host to the backpack rap set wearing Baby Phat, Ecko, and Adidas originals. We paid our ten-dollar cover charge and were shunted out onto an open dance floor where b-boys genuflected midpose before the religious icons and stained-glass windows that adorned the space.

I was immediately struck by the diversity of the faces. In one cypher a slim Asian woman came out of a freeze and conceded the floor to a black guy in dreads, who rocked upright for a few moments and then dropped to the floor in a characteristic six-step routine. Beyond my friend Gautam, who is Indian, and Mike, an Irish American from Chicago's South Side, I saw other

Asian Americans, African Americans, whites, and Latinos. I had been strongly drawn to the multiracial nature of Chicago as a city, and this dance club seemed to be an expression of that.

Taking in the scene, I wondered if these multiracial b-boys and b-girls were a product of Chicago's underground hip hop resurgence. I had followed the rise of underground independent rap in places like the San Francisco Bay Area, where the rap artist Too Short's albums went gold and platinum without major label support. The Chicago artists Common, Twista, and Kanye West followed suit soon after. In contrast to the stereotypical and violent representations of blackness in corporate rap—consumed by mostly white suburban audiences—underground rap made room for different ethnicities, different ways of being black, and other alternatives to the standard music industry formulas.[1] Maybe underground rap could be the vehicle for uniting the hip hop generation, bringing it together across racial and ethnic lines.

Yet how, I thought as I crossed the dance floor to the bar, could these brown and white faces find a place within the imagined black planet? In Cuba rappers were Afro-descendant; their claims to blackness were undisputed, at least within hip hop. But if hip hop was an essentially black cultural form, as scholars such as Tricia Rose and later Imani Perry argued, then on what grounds did hip hoppers of other races claim to belong?

It's hard to understand much about race or hip hop in Chicago without visiting the South Side—the predominantly working-class part of the city populated by large numbers of blacks and Latinos. My chance came just a week after my trans-Pacific relocation—after my initial Cuban sojourn, I had briefly returned home to Sydney to prepare for my move to Chicago. I moved into an unfurnished apartment in the university neighborhood of Hyde Park before the semester started at the University of Chicago. Mike suggested that I come by his parents' house on the South Side to pick up a mattress that I could sleep on.

I caught a bus from Hyde Park and then switched to the "L" train. As the train went on its aboveground route, I looked out of the window at the landscape. We passed burned-out carcasses of buildings, empty lots surrounded by barbed wire and overgrown with weeds, and boarded-up storefronts.

The train whizzed by scores of graffiti pieces and tags. The veteran graffiti writer William Upski Wimsatt recounts in his book *Bomb the Suburbs* that hip hop culture in Chicago had some rocky beginnings. In 1974 a crew of New York City graffiti writers had a meeting with the Chicago gang Blackstone Rangers to introduce its members to graffiti. But the gang youth were not so interested.[2] It wasn't until about 1982 that graffiti took off in Chicago, with artists such as CTA, Car Crew, Trixter, and ABC Crew.

Between 1985 and 1987 the rooftops along the CTA (Chicago Transit Authority) train lines were the focus of graffiti art. In 1987 Trixter and the ABC Crew began to paint trains like their counterparts in New York City and elsewhere, bombing entire lines like the Congress Line. In 1989 the area north of Chinatown became a hot spot for graffiti with the Wall of Fame around the Eighteenth Street railroad.[3] As Wimsatt recalls, sessions at the Wall of Fame were often preceded by all-city writers' meetings attended by upward of eighty kids, in an effort to unite crews across the city.[4]

B-boying had started in the mid- to late 1970s, with crews such as Down to Rock, Krazy Krew, and the Windy City Breakers. In 1978 Lord Cashus D started a chapter of Afrika Bambaataa's Universal Zulu Nation in Chicago. In 1990, together with Geoffrey Watts and Aaron Brown, Cashus D created a hip hop organization called the New World Order that flourished briefly and then died out. The political and organizational efforts of Chicago hip hop pioneers were linked to the city's history of militant units that included street gangs, the Nation of Islam, and the Black Panthers. Hip hop meetings—with the first held in the Cabrini Green housing projects in 1985 by a high school senior named Warp—were a distinctly Chicago phenomenon and one of several efforts to organize the disparate Chicago scene.[5]

I got off at the Ashland and Sixty-third Street stop, and Mike was waiting there in his parents' beat-up, gun-metal gray 1993 Dodge Caravan.

As we drove the few blocks along Sixty-third Street to Kedzie, Mike explained that the black population of the South Side had migrated from the rural South during the early and midtwentieth century to work in the steel mills and meatpacking plants. They were housed in tightly cramped conditions in the South Side's Black Belt and later in public housing projects such as the Trumbull Park Homes, Dearborn Homes, and the Robert Taylor Homes. But by the 1980s the industrial base of the South Side was in decline as meatpacking companies and steel factories, such as Wisconsin Steel and US Steel's South Works, closed down. Large sectors of the South Side turned to urban wasteland. Whites fled to the suburbs. Small businesses shut down. Banks foreclosed on people's homes. And through all this hardship, the city administrations cut back spending on public services and infrastructure.

"The Chicago authorities just allowed the communities to decay and die," said Mike. "There are no good grocery stores. There are liquor stores everywhere." He motioned around us. "Just after white people started to run like hell from the black folks, that opened up housing and Mexican people moved in to this area, too. It's unique to Chicago as well, since Chicago is extraordinarily segregated, and this is one of the few areas where you have Mexican and African American communities living together with the small remnant Irish American community."

Chicago was segregated. The North Side of Chicago and the suburbs were very white. The South Side and West Side were mostly black and Latino. Each ethnic group had its own separate enclave. The melting pot didn't seem to extend much beyond cross-sampling of cuisines or music—blues at the Checkerboard Lounge on the South Side, kalamata olives in Greektown, Dim Sum in Chinatown, or a dosa in the South Asian neighborhood of Devon. Public spaces were also divided by race. When I went to the University of Chicago to enroll in my classes for the fall, I noticed that many of the students, professors, and visitors to the university were white. The staff serving food in the cafeterias and unloading boxes, the janitors, and security guards were almost all black. While I was at the university, a black graduate student friend was mistaken for a member of the cleaning staff in the student housing where she lived. A city could be multiracial and racially divided at the same time. But could music overcome these kinds of entrenched barriers and help people to see beyond the bubbles in which they lived?

I gazed out the window of the van. Most of the store signs along Kedzie were in Spanish: Envios de Dinero, Fotos: Bodas y Quinceaneras, Tamales. There were auto parts stores, Mexican restaurants with cartoons of cacti and men in sombreros, a dollar store with its sign half ripped off, and the ubiquitous liquor stores. A kid with a do-rag on his head cruised along the sidewalk on his bike. One sign read in bold red lettering: "Sell your property in 30 days!!" A thrift store was boarded up with a "For Sale" sign posted outside.

We pulled into Sixty-second Place and Mike parked the car outside his parents' modest brick house. His mom lay asleep on the couch, a movie blaring on the television screen. We tiptoed past her. "She works night shifts as a nurse, so most days this is how she falls asleep."

We chatted over cans of Coke in the kitchen. Mike had grown up on the South Side. He came of age in the mid-1980s at the height of the crack epidemic.

"There wasn't a tremendous amount of jobs to be had when I was growing up," Mike explained. "We all had our share of shit jobs at factories, and mowing people's lawns, and low-paid service work. But we also had our own alternative economies, like stealing and selling things at Maxwell Street."[6]

Along with other kids in the neighborhood, Mike became involved with the b-boy craze of the '80s. "It was just something we did out on the street," said Mike. "If you were sitting on the curb, and somebody came along and you didn't have a tape or a box and they did, they'd stop, you'd run in to get your cardboard, and then soon people would gather. We never established a proper crew. It was much more fluid than that, and I think that's how most blocks were. It was like baseball—pick-up. You'd just be sitting on the curb, and people would come by and you'd start playing, same as b-boying."

"Run-DMC was huge back then in the early eighties," Mike reminisced. "We had a cheap-ass turntable and this really cheap tape recorder, and I would put the microphone by the speaker on the turntable and record the shit off the vinyl to the tape, just so we would have a tape for the box when we would break. By the end of the summer those tapes were just worn through."

Jermaine was an older guy from Mike's neighborhood. "This dude had a huge box that was like the size of a coffee table," Mike recalled, "and he was a big dude so he could carry it around all over the place. He always had the latest music and he would have it on tape. He would bring it to school. He was huge—he was like Raheem from *Do the Right Thing*. He was later run over and killed by a cop. He was a great guy and everybody loved him; he was a real part of everybody's breakin.' He was the spark that initiated hip hop and brought it to a younger generation. He was part of the community, and it was a real tremendous shock when he was killed purposefully by the police. That was never investigated. I don't think anybody was ever arrested for his death."

The early history of hip hop culture on the South Side, like life in general, was connected to gangs and their control of the territory. Mike explained: "The two main gang alliances in Chicago were Folks and People, just like the Bloods and Crips of LA. The gangs were involved with drug trafficking and grand theft, and the gangs made it possible to unite and operate a tight system to get around the police structure. They also contributed to building the community. That doesn't mean it's rosy growing up in a neighborhood where the gang is controlling your streets, because as a kid they want you in. If you're in, it means you're protected, but you also have a tremendous responsibility to that gang. If you're not in, you can still work with them and gain some protection from rival gangs, which is what I did. I had seen friends in gangs being killed or committed to a life in prison. Despite the stability of the gang's presence, it was still very tenuous, and to commit everything to that was pretty scary. But it's also pretty

scary to be on your own. Our area was controlled by the Gangster Disciples, one of Chicago's most notorious gangs, and Two
Six, which comes from the name Twenty-sixth Street, a Mexican
gang which came down from Pilsen and moved south. They
were both part of the Folk Nation, so our area was controlled by
the Folks when I was growing up."

On Chicago's South Side graffiti art was strongly tied to gangs'
establishing territory and communicating events and murders.
To go over someone else's tag could have dire consequences.
As Mike related, "I was not a tagger growing up because I was
scared that I'd fuck around and piss somebody off and, next
thing I know, I'd be getting shot. Graffiti definitely had a different context in terms of the gangs.

"The beautiful thing about hip hop was that it really gave you
a sense of your own humanity in the midst of seeing and expe-
riencing some truly horrible shit," he concluded. "Where we
grew up, it was like living in a war zone. That kind of traumatic
experience. And hip hop really infused your common everyday
experience with new life and even hope. For many of my friends
it didn't translate into a real hope; it was fleeting. A lot of them
are dead, a lot of them are in jail. I'm the only one who made it
out. I had a stability that others didn't have, like two parents and
step-parents who could pool their income to pay for my education and eventually get me out of there."

We loaded the mattress into Mike's parents' van, and he
drove me back to Hyde Park. With the start of the school year,
and our busy lives, it would be another year or so before our
paths crossed again. On that evening I had little inkling that
Mike would turn out to be my future husband.

I was keen to find out more about Chicago hip hop, especially
its underground scene, but living in Hyde Park made this kind
of exploration difficult. Hyde Park was an island of privilege on
the South Side. During the 1950s and 1960s the University of
Chicago had carried out an urban renewal project in Hyde Park
in an attempt to create a middle-class white community in the
heart of the Black Belt. The university used its neighborhood

redevelopment corporation to evict black tenants, leading to tensions with the surrounding black community. But the results were mixed. Years later there were still large black populations residing in the areas of northwestern Hyde Park adjoining the ghetto, while the immediate vicinity of the university was owned mostly by whites.[7]

The university expended much energy on controlling who entered the area. Public transportation out of Hyde Park was possible in the evenings, but bus services into the area stopped around 8 o'clock. The university didn't want any undesirables coming in on the Jeffrey 6 bus. Our email accounts were bombarded by frequent crime watch and safety warnings. We were cautioned not to be out alone past 9 p.m.

Student organizations on campus encountered resistance from the university's administration when they wanted to bring in rap bands touring on the college circuits. When the administration finally relented and allowed the iconoclastic rap act Black Eyed Peas to do a show on the lawns adjacent to the dining commons, there was a strict system of security set up to keep out any local residents. Students had to show their ID to enter. As a somewhat bored will.i.am entered the stage before a lackluster crowd of college kids, a line of armed security was suddenly visible on the nearby roofs and perimeters of the event. Were they worried the show might awaken the unbridled passions of an engineering student? Or, God forbid, that it might attract actual black people?

Knowing my frustrations with Hyde Park, my friend Anurima Bhargava introduced me to her former classmate and local rapper Mike Treese. One day we stopped by Café Florian, a Hyde Park bar and restaurant where Treese worked night shifts as a delivery person. Treese was a shy white guy who wore a baseball cap pulled down low. With a black rapper, Gee Field, Treese formed a rap duo known as Mass Hysteria. Anurima and Treese had both gone to Kenwood High in Hyde Park, which had produced the rapper Da Brat and the R&B singer R. Kelly. When Treese gave me a ride to Anurima's New Year's Eve party later that week, we revealed our initial suspicions about the other. "When I first saw you, I was, like, what would she know about hip hop?" he admitted to me. "Well, when I saw you," I replied, "I was thinking, how can this white boy make it as a rapper?"

Treese told me about his life growing up in Hyde Park and going to a mostly black public school. It seemed that a by-product of the university's gentrification efforts was the creation of some new integrated spaces in a highly segregated city, as Treese experienced growing up. And these integrated spaces—much like Mike Walsh had described in the case of his South Side community—did provide some opportunity for blacks and whites to come together through hip hop culture. It struck me how the whites who participated in hip hop culture generally invoked their atypical life experiences—they were born in a black area or grew up in the projects or went to a black school. It was their pain, their poverty, or their truncated life options that made them identify with hip hop. And as S. Craig Watkins has said, white poverty in America has largely been invisible, as it violates dominant notions about race and class.[8] White rappers like Treese weaved these details into their narratives, as if being white meant you had more to prove.

"My life—to use a Jay-Z line—was both a 'gift and a curse.' In fact, I thought of that line before him," Treese said. Some of Treese's family members suffered drug and alcohol addictions, and he himself struggled with depression. Only, his escape was music rather than alcohol or drugs. "The best thing my parents ever did for me was put me in public schools in Hyde Park, because they didn't have enough money to send me to private school. For Chicago to be the most segregated city in the country, I grew up in the most integrated community, which was Hyde Park. That's where I was introduced to hip hop."

As one of the few white kids in his school, Treese grew up feeling like he was in the wrong place at the wrong time. "As a white kid going to a black school, you're really just tryin' to fit in," he recalled. "I was a shy, skinny-ass kid. Not just being a white kid among all black people but a really little kid who was a late bloomer with everything. So you felt like you had to play catch-up and compete even harder 'cause you were little. That defined my life. I had a fear of being left out. Nobody wants to be the last kid picked on the team. Nobody wants to get their ass whipped. And for a little kid, nobody ever fucked with me."

But it was by being on the South Side that he was introduced to hip hop. "The fact is that I heard 'Jam on It' when that came out," recalled Treese, "and I was break-dancing to it. I remember this one kid, Donald, would have a boom box, and he would tape shit off the radio, and we would practice to that. And I heard Run-DMC's first rap songs. I heard 'Roxanne Roxanne' and 'Rappin' Duke.' I remember buying *Raising Hell* on my own, I remember buying *License to Ill* on my own. My older brother had friends, and they would have boom boxes and play 'Din Da Da' and 'Planet Rock.' We didn't know where this shit came from. I remember even in eighty-seven when *Paid in Full* came out, we was looking at the tape, like, which one do you think is Eric B and which one do you think is Rakim? We didn't know—nobody had cable and videos. You saw that later on. We didn't experience it like New York kids. I didn't really see people rapping till high school. But in grammar school there were definitely people break-dancing on cardboard, and graffiti was prevalent."

Mike Treese of Mass Hysteria

© Ronnie Boykin

© Samantha Robinson

Gee Field of Mass Hysteria

In Treese's senior year of high school, rap culture was at its peak. "I used to write rhymes here and there but not seriously till my senior year in high school," Treese recalled. "Everything in my high school and in Chicago in ninety-two was hip hop. There was still other shit that existed. There was still gangster culture, and House culture, but hip hop exploded in that year. It's never exploded like that since then or before then. That's when I met the people that I got down with, like Gee Field. They realized that they were serious about it too, so we could do something together."

Gee Field was a classmate of Treese's, hailing from a rough South Shore neighborhood known as Terror Town. Gee was born at Seventy-sixth and Walcott on the Southwest Side and moved to South Shore with his mother and siblings after she separated from his father—the well-known old-school R&B singer Garland Green. During his father's studio sessions in their basement, Gee had met Michael Jackson and other celebrities. Gee's mom would play old-school hip hop like Sugar Hill Gang on the radio in the car.

In the mid-1980s, when he was in grade school, Gee had a classmate who introduced him to the rap show on the

University of Chicago radio station WHPK. "It didn't come on until 12 o'clock midnight," Gee related. "Sure 'nuff, I stayed up and I listened to the show and it just opened up a whole new world for me. There was this DJ named JP Chill who played mostly New York hip hop, it was really bubblin' at the time. He'd play uncensored versions, curse words. I had these tapes called Tone-Master tapes. I would pop one in my cassette deck, 'cause I could probably only stay up for the first hour of the three-hour show. After about twelve-thirty or one, my mom would peek in and see me messing around. She'd say, 'Boy, get yourself to bed,' and hit me upside the head. I would sneak the tape in before I went to bed."

Mike Treese and Gee were participants in the citywide hip hop meetings in the early 1990s. "We used to throw hip hop meetings," Treese explained, "and you could only come to the meeting if you did one of the four elements. You couldn't just come if you were a fan, 'cause we had been fans our whole life. Now it's, like, we're eighteen—now we gotta do something serious. So are you a b-boy? You a graffiti writer? You a rapper? You a DJ? You a producer? So you had to do something. There'd be like a hundred of us. We used to meet up on the train tracks, and we called it the 'heat box' on the Metra tracks. It was, like, a glass-enclosed place where you wait for the train. We'd just meet up there, and some of us rapping, kids doing graffiti, then people start breakin'. So that was ninety-two, that was our *Beat Street*. But it didn't last, 'cause that's the time you have to make grownup decisions. Most graffiti writers don't make any money. Most b-boys don't make any money. If you're lucky as a DJ or a rapper, you might make money here or there. Ninety-two was the year Common came out. Twista came out. A lot of people's careers got started back then, including me. Back then you could look at it, like, well, OK, Common and Twista got deals, so maybe we can, too. But the shit didn't work like that."

The underground independent route began to develop in Chicago around the midnineties as an alternative to the major labels that came to dominate the music industry. One event that gave impetus to Chicago's underground was the buyout of the twenty-four-hour hip hop radio station WJPC 950 AM in the summer of 1994. It became 106 Jamz and switched to the generic formula of New York's Hot 97.[9] The monopoly of the media giant Clear Channel Communications over a large majority of radio stations—following the loosening of restrictions on media ownership in the Telecommunications Act of 1996—meant that radio playlists became much more formulaic in general. Airtime became a commodity for sale, and independent artists who couldn't afford to pay for it had no chance of having their songs on the air.

Live Nation—a spin-off of Clear Channel Communications—owned SFX Entertainment, which managed a large number of the country's entertainment venues. Corporate monopoly over entertainment venues contributed to the exclusion of independent artists. The Chicago House of Blues—acquired by Live Nation in 2006—was unwilling to showcase local rap artists, even as opening acts for the national rap acts regularly touring Chicago. Even before the takeover by Live Nation, the venue was accused of being exclusionary. In April 2000 the hip hop community organized a large demonstration outside the House of Blues. According to the protesters, the House of Blues marketed itself as a historic venue for preserving black and Latino culture. They alleged that the venue prevented urban youth from getting their events in, and quoted local artists exorbitant prices for nonprime slots. The House of Blues regularly booked national rap acts like 50 Cent or Nelly with restrictively high prices for the tickets. Some local artists invoked the situation of jazz in the 1920s, when clubs booked black acts while excluding black audiences.

The major labels were signing artists with club appeal, danceable music, and the standard formula of bragging about women, cars, and money. It may have been possible to get a hit song on the radio without being signed to a major label, but this meant buying beats from producers who consistently had hit songs, which meant shelling out close to $200,000 for a beat. Or it just meant getting lucky and being a one-hit wonder. Neither route was sufficient to sustain a career and an artist for the long term.

Even making it gold or platinum on a label once didn't guarantee a sustainable income if the artist couldn't continue to produce a sound that sold commercially.

Since commercial radio was out of the question, the main resources for independent hip hop artists were college radio stations, as well as small local venues and retail. This combination was enough to sustain the careers of underground artists in, for example, the San Francisco Bay Area. The retail support of small record stores along Telegraph Avenue in Berkeley, mini-chain stores such as Rasputin, and college and community radio stations could allow independent artists in the Bay Area to sell up to fifteen thousand CDs locally.

But in Chicago many of the mom-and-pop stores were bought out by national chains such as Best Buy. College radio stations such as WHPK had three hip hop shows a week, but the audiences were so small that they couldn't really be used by artists to promote their sales. Despite this, there still existed a large enough community of people in Chicago who didn't want to listen to the major radio formula and who supported independent hip hop. Here in Chicago, it seemed I had stumbled upon a real, authentic underground that wasn't looking for handouts from the government or kudos from the market to make its music.

There was a long line outside Double Door for the Monday hip hop night, but the bouncer waved us straight in, no cover charge. I was with my girls. Nicole was a Trinidadian American from Brooklyn who was a fellow grad student. Anurima was a desi who had grown up on the South Side close to Hyde Park. Hip hop night tended to be mainly guys, and in an attempt to attract more females the organizers had the ten-dollar cover charge waived for those of our gender.

Double Door was in the bohemian, gentrifying northwestern neighborhood of Wicker Park. There was a concentration of clubs in this area and farther north as well, in the whiter neighborhoods. Hip hoppers from the South Side and West Side had to come north to access the club scene. In earlier periods like the 1940s and 1950s, black entrepreneurs and blues and jazz musicians had propelled a vibrant entertainment circuit of cafes, nightclubs, and musical theater on Chicago's South Side and West Side. But with the economic crisis spurred by deindustrialization, most of these entertainment venues were shut down, with the exception of a few blues clubs that still attracted tourists.

On the North Side, hip hoppers had to struggle for spaces and venues. During a dry spell in the mid-1980s, they used to b-boy in the House clubs to keep their form alive.[10] Rap promoters faced stigma and hostility from white managers at the upscale North Side venues who associated rap music with crime, violence, and gangs. Other venues just didn't see revenue coming from the young and financially challenged hip hop audiences. "Hip hop nights" had become one means for Chicago hip hoppers to gather and perform. The first open mic night was organized by Duro Wicks at the Lizard Lounge in the Ukranian Village in 1991.[11] It was known as the one-dollar Sunday hip hop show. After that ended (as Wicks said in an interview, "It was just too black for the club and they let us go"), promoters and DJs began to host hip hop nights at other venues like Lower Links, Elbo Room, Double Door, and Subterranean. The hip hop night at Double Door—dubbed the "Bluegroove Lounge"—was started by the DJ Jesse De La Pena at the Elbo Room in 1994 and cohosted by Spo and Dirty MF. The DJs Pumpin' Pete, aka Supacuts, 33 1/3, and Nonstop would also spin at Double Door on hip hop night.

I caught up with Jesse sometime later, and he told me his story. Of mixed Irish, German, and Mexican descent, Jesse was raised on Chicago's Southeast Side by his single mother. When he was a teenager, they moved to the Southwest Side. He was into graffiti and break dancing and had a few friends who were DJs. He watched them and listened to their tapes, and then decided that he wanted to be a DJ. Since hip hop was not big at that time, an older DJ friend would pass along all his hip hop promo records to Jesse. Jesse listened to WHPK and other college radio stations—which were the only ones at the time playing hip hop—and then he would buy the music he heard on the radio.

In high school Jesse saved up and bought a Technics 1200 turntable from a friend. He also had an all-in-one stereo player with a turntable on the top, so he started figuring out how to DJ using the knobs. He would turn the volume up and down like a fader on a mixer. He made a scratch pad out of an old album cover. Then, as he improved his skills, he got a mixer and eventually a second turntable. It was also a Technics 1200, pretty beat-up. The tone arm was cracked and Krazy-Glued back together; when it periodically fell off, Jesse reattached it with rubber bands.

As a DJ, Jesse had nowhere to spin hip hop. He lost a lot of early gigs playing hip hop. He relates that "when I started to spin it, everybody, including black folk, would leave the floor. Nobody was feeling it." So he started out playing House, new wave, and industrial music at parties in clubs, basements, and warehouses for half-hour sets.

"At that point there were occasional hip hop events or concerts," Jesse recalled. "I remember going to the Fresh Fest at the UIC pavilion [University of Chicago, Illinois] in 1985 or '86. It featured Whodini, Grandmaster Flash, and a bunch of other hip hop groups. I also saw Run-DMC and the Beastie Boys in concert. There were hip hop parties like Steps up north or the Blue Gargoyle on the South Side, but they all came and went, they never really lasted. So I was looking for somewhere that me and all my friends—who were DJs and b-boys and graffiti artists—could showcase our talents. The idea of doing a weekly hip hop night was really just a networking and a community thing. We started off at the Elbo Room, and then as it grew we needed a bigger location. Double Door just seemed to make sense because of its size and location—bigger stage, better sound system. We just outgrew the Elbo Room."

We entered the main floor of the club. There were a few scattered tables, with a large open area and a stage. The audience was mostly urban black youth—a mixture of aspiring rappers and b-boys up from the South Side and West Side, and some college students. This demographic would change dramatically in years to come, when the underground audiences would become largely white. Along one side of the club was a narrow fluorescent bar. But most of the crowd was focused on the cypher that had opened in the center of the floor. One after another, b-boys entered the ring. They warmed up with a few quick circular steps. Then they dropped to the floor and executed head spins, legs and arms whipping through the air, then balanced precariously in a freeze, while the crowd cheered them on. After a while a second cypher opened up, and people migrated over to see if they were missing anything there.

Jesse spun old-school records for a while, original soul, jazz, and rock, followed by an open mic. It was a trial by fire from a tough crowd that knew what it liked and what it didn't. The open mic scene pushed Chicago rappers to hone their skills and their stage presence. They weren't just studio rappers; they could work a crowd.[12] There was a certain buzz in the air because some big underground acts would make an appearance in the show tonight.

"Let's see some crowd participation," the rapper Capital D of All Natural primed the audience, and a few people shouted back. "Do we keep it hard core?" he asked. "Hell, yeah," the audience responded.

"Underground, straight raw, do the heads want more?"

"Hell, yeah!" the audience screamed.

"Do the heads want more?"

"HELL, YEAH!"

Over a minimal beat, with recorded scratching from DJ Tone B Nimble, Capital D rapped in a low voice,

> Take it back to the days before b-boys was gettin' blown away
> And sons was livin' off the props of their pops like Nona Gaye[13]
> But the pendulum will sway, and you're gonna pay
> Will I be bopping to the beats that Tone'll play?
> It's the only way, of course some will say that that's the lonely way
> But hey, I'd rather stand on my own
> Than be a puppet with a string on a microphone.

Then the riff, an underground anthem: "Now do we keep it hard core? / Underground, straight, raw / On tour, we're going from shore to shore, now do you heads want more? / Yo, do we keep it hard core?"

After All Natural, Mass Hysteria was on the stage. Over the speakers, there was a heavy bass with a high-pitched buzzing, like a swarm of insects or police sirens on alert. Treese was rapping over the top:

> No one made you do this,
> Would you stay true to this, if you weren't paid to do this
> So stop bragging about your number one hit
> I thought you knew, my crew don't care about that dumb shit.
> I'm not one of you, not like you, none of you, not even some
>   of you
> Dis me, what will become of you, you'll be gone, for good.
> My life don't mean shit to me, tell me why the fuck you think
>   yours would.

Then more scratching and the hook to the song: "On the mike, I let vocabulary spill," repeated over and over.

I was gratified to see a woman up next—Angela Zone, aka Ang 13. Underground hip hop in Chicago tended to be a male affair. Ang 13's background beat, by the veteran Chi-town hip hop producers the Molemen, opened with the tones of a piano and synthesized violins. "I'll take you back in time, the year is '89," 13 opened her rhyme, a personal narrative about her troubled relationship with her parents. "It was moms who brung this / Sit back, I'm gonna tell ya how my peeps and I swung it." The song recounts 13's trips to the emergency room as a young child, her dad off with another woman, then her mom in jail while Ang 13 and her sister were raised by relatives.

"Moms had a lot of male friends who I detested," 13 continued, "running in and out, then one night I got molested / Never talked to me about the incident as if it never happened / All I heard was her in the next room / It never got better, worst came to worst / Before she looked out for her kids, she always looked out for her man first." On the chorus she rhymed, "You

Ang 13

understand what it's like now / I hate their ways, yet I love 'em / Never will forgive my moms, she put my sister out at 18 / But first she tried to break her fuckin' arm / So many times I wanted to flex / But I knew I had to watch my neck, 'cause I knew that my ass would be next."

Finally, as an adult, 13 reconciles with her mom. "'I'm sorry, forgive me / I love you, I never meant to snub you,' said moms / Said how she was dead wrong / *Sad songs say so much*, don't know how she hurt me so much / Situation made me go nuts." These personal and raw narratives of women's experiences were something that was absent in corporate rap—but they were also surprisingly rare in underground rap. It was also unusual to see women up at the open mic. Given underground rappers' polemic against the one-dimensional "bitches, hoes, and bling bling" formula, I thought that this scene would create more spaces for women, queers, and those generally outside the orbit of commercial rap. Why didn't that seem to be the case?

The final act for the night was the renowned freestyle battle rapper Che Smith, aka Rhymefest. Fest hailed from the far South Side neighborhood of South Deering and had come to fame the previous year, when at seventeen he and his rapping partner, Terrence Parker, aka MC Juice, had beaten the notable white rapper Eminem in an emcee battle at the Scribble Jam.

The track consisted of synthesized horns and bells leading into a sparse beat. "Well, hey, yo," rapped Fest, over the top of the beat. He looked over to Juice. "What's up, Juice, it's about time that we set it straight and show these other cities how to represent and regulate / Y'all niggas don't want to spark me / I can hit the rhythm 'n' split 'em just from the drums of my heart beat / Yo, I can't deny I live and die for the streets of Chi / But there's more than meets the eye, than pimpin' hoes and getting' high / You do or die, but you can live and do the same thing."

Juice entered, "No pause or comma, 'cause I'm gonna keep you fearin' this / You got a question mark, I'm the nigga here, period."

"Dope it is."

"I am."

"But can you rock?"

"I can."

"You think ya dope."

"I do."

"That's how we chill, part two."

Juice continued:

Versace wearing rappers, always tryna play some pimps in this
   biz,
These record labels sign the most unpresentable
Hits that go platinum for grabbin' on their genitals
And every single day brothas is dyin' in my mix,
But all they ever rap about is Alize and grabbin' dicks.
Now you might say who is Juice to try to check sombody else,
But it do get kinda boring always rappin' 'bout yourself
And your jewelry and your guns, you think that shit is rhymin'?
The billboards say you climbin' but every trend has its timing
I ain't sayin' no names, but why you bitin' his style
I'll have all you niggas layin' in the casket with your Cristal

There was a certain reality to underground rappers' beef with corporate capitalism. It wasn't theoretical, as in the case of the Cuban rappers who experienced capitalism by long distance. It came from years of winning Scribble Jam battles and still working low-wage jobs or from seeing countless young black men in the 'hood hoping to get rich and dying trying. If underground rappers sounded bitter and cynical, it came from seeing the meteoric rise of those willing to embrace the music industry formulas, while their years of "paying dues" by studying and nurturing the culture with scarce resources counted for naught in the marketplace of MTV.

It was a Tuesday night at Subterranean, and a sizable crowd had gathered to see Chicago's finest hip hop DJs. The attention of the audience was focused on Johnny Cervantes, aka DJ Presyce, who had worked with Mass Hysteria and had been a part of crews the Molemen and Turntable Technicians. DJ Presyce was a round-faced Mexican American guy who grew up on the South Side at Sixty-third and California. When he was fourteen, Presyce and his older brother Jesus, or "Chuy," watched tapes from the annual DJ competition known as the DMC World DJ Championships, and they taught themselves how to scratch. Chuy was a car mechanic, and he and Presyce mastered the inner machinery of their turntables by taking them apart and then putting them back together.

Presyce won the DJ battle at the Cincinnati-based Scribble Jam contest three years in a row before being forced to retire from the competition. In 1998 he participated in a regional DMC DJ battle, winning a spot in the US finals, where he came in second in 2002. But being a dope battle DJ didn't really translate into money, and Presyce was working at Best Buy and Target to get by.

The earnest audience at Subterranean—consisting of mostly male DJs, emcees, and fans—filled the cocktail tables at the front and center of the room. People were focused intently on the turntables, appraising every move of the DJ. Others were drinking and talking quietly on the sides and at the back of the club on velvet couches. It was very different from a typical club scene, where people got drunk, flirted with each other, and shouted over the din of the music. Here all attention was on the DJ at the front.

Presyce was just getting warmed up at his instrument. One hand was scratching the record on the left turntable back and forth. The other flew deftly over the mixer, manipulating the crossfader and volume control at a dizzying pace.

A few young women—most of them girlfriends of the DJs—were clustered together at the back. As I sat with Mike Treese at one of the cocktail tables at the front, it struck me that this was yet another segregated space. But rather than being divided by skin color, it was divided by gender. There was a masculine camaraderie among the DJs, rappers, and producers who populated the front of the club. They all read the same magazines, debated the origins of a particular sample, shared information about rare record auctions, and watched classic DJ battle videos at each other's crib. The women at the back were excluded from this society because they didn't have the right cultural knowledge to be a part of it, or they self-excluded because they weren't that interested. I felt like an interloper among the males—I really didn't have much of an opinion on the difference in sound quality between an SR-16 drum machine and a Roland TR-808.

The show was under way. Presyce was manipulating the record on the right to speed it up till the voices on it began to sound like squeaky cartoon characters, and then he slowed it down to produce the droning effect of an old tape. Audience members were on the edge of their seats. As he quickened and slowed the pace of the record on the right, he always kept it in time with the record he was scratching on the left, with the mathematical calculation that had earned him his DJ name.

There was still something else about the underground that fostered such a closed culture. The underground had been fighting so long and hard against the perversions of the music industry that it became obsessed with its own purity, even at times to the exclusion of what was different. It brought to mind Randy's evocation of "rice with mango" to describe the fusion rap denigrated by the Cuban underground. The melding with other musical genres and styles was perceived by the underground as an encroachment, even though hip hop since its birth had always been nourished by other traditions and would probably live on in different musical forms. But here and now what mattered was dedication to the art form, practicing your lyrical or acrobatic or digital dexterity. While the outside world—including maybe your family and former schoolmates—saw you as a pizza deliverer or Target employee, the underground recognized your genius. This was one place where hip hop still held to high standards. It was just that sometimes those high standards translated into conformity.

After the show Treese and I drove back to Hyde Park in his black '94 Jetta, with leather seats that heated up in the winter. I told him that I would really like to start performing again but that I felt insecure about whether I would be accepted. "Dude," he looked over from the wheel with incredulity on his face. "If I have to work this hard to get people to take me seriously as a white emcee, how are they gonna accept an Indian female emcee with an Australian accent!"

Yo, just calling to let you know that our new joint is out. I'm coming by to drop off a copy for you." On the phone Treese sounded excited.

It was April 2000, and it had been a while since I had seen Treese. He and Gee Field were busy in the studio recording their latest album, and I would finally get to hear it.

Treese lugged a suitcase up the stairs to my fourth-floor apartment. It was full of CDs and he pulled one out for me. The cover was a color photocopy with the name of the album—*Cooley High: Class of 2000*—and images of two characters from the cult film *Cooley High*, the Chicago version of *Wildstyle*. The playlist consisted of tracks from well-known Chicago artists like All Natural, Juice, Common, Vakil, and Prime Meridian, together with songs from Mass Hysteria. It was a classic mixtape, a hip hop staple that dated from the early days when DJs would record shows and then sell the tapes in order to promote themselves. It didn't matter that this wasn't an actual four-track tape, because the idea of the mixtape—as a do-it-yourself artifact—still reigned in the era of CDs. I turned on the CD player and popped it in.

There was a sound of someone knocking on a door, then a raspy voice, "What the hell you want here, honky?" "I'm, uh, looking … Is Louise here?" "There's no goddamn Louise live here, honky." "But, I—" Then the sound of a door slamming. A realization, "My money—" Then in a higher pitch, "I've been screwed!" It was a sample from *Cooley High*, a scene from the film where some neighborhood guys find a white man at the local bar and promise him that he can have sex with a prostitute named Louise.[14] They drop him off at an unidentified location, offer to guard his belongings, and then take off with all his possessions while he's upstairs knocking at the door. It's all about the hustle.

The next track was an interlude, with scratching by Presyce and short stabs of synthesized keyboards. KRS and Method Man repeated "Mass Hysteria, Mass Hysteria," in sampled clips and then the female emcee Rage, rhyming "Always and forever," intermixed with various other samples from Xzibit and Pete Rock.

"So how do you sell these? Concerts? Mom-and-pop stores? Word of mouth?" I was curious.

"I mostly sell these myself at concerts and parties," Treese explained. "But the problem with Chicago is, 'cause it's so segregated and spread out, you have to drive a lot. The West Side is a whole different world. If you're doing hip hop shit, you are not gonna sell on the West Side, period. And the West Side shit is not gonna sell on the North Side. So you gotta go to Evanston, then you gotta go to the south suburbs, then you gotta go to the west suburbs, Hyde Park."

Treese described what a night of selling mixtapes would look like. He might leave his crib around 11 p.m. He would drive to a concert, maybe a rap show at the House of Blues, even though he didn't have a ticket. Then he would pitch his CD to people waiting in line or even inside the show, if he could make it in. His pitch would include drawing the person's attention to the big names on the playlist, highlighting the quality of the mixtape compared to what other DJs were putting out, and then talking about Mass Hysteria. It might take several pitches before he could sell a CD. These were the days before music downloads, podcasts, and iTunes, and people often bought the CD because they wouldn't have access to the music otherwise—not unless they bought 12-inch singles on a regular basis. Sometimes he would get spotted by security, and when he failed to produce a ticket, he would be escorted out from the building. If the show was in full swing, it left few people outside to sell to. He would have to wait outside until the show was over, and he could begin selling to people as they left. In one night of hustling he might sell fourteen CDs at ten dollars a pop. After calculating $70 of that in overhead, that's $70 profit. For five hours of work, that's about $12 an hour.

"Last winter I got sick three times just from being out in the cold," Treese sighed. "But I still kept going out and selling CDs. You can push it better on your own than giving it to a record store. You gotta do your pitch in order to sell your records."

I nodded and thought back to my rapper friends in Cuba who complained that the state didn't record or distribute their music. Here in Chicago, rappers like Treese were trying to do it on their own, but they came up against so many obstacles. Being an independent artist was much harder than I had imagined. Success and failure are all on you as an artist. "I paid dues," rapped Gee Field on one of the tracks, "but if I don't make it, then who tha fuck'll reimburse me?"

"I once read somewhere that being a street-level drug dealer is a low-wage job," Treese reflected, "when you figure out how much he makes versus how much time he has to spend doing it. For the time you're putting into it, it's not worth it. It's the same way with independent rap and selling shit on your own. It's hard. It's time consuming. Maybe I'll make one hundred dollars on a night, maybe two or three hundred dollars on a good night. But that's from going to three or four different clubs and bars and staying out from at least 11 p.m. to getting home at 4 a.m. That's a shift. I mean that's work, like going to a restaurant and working for five hours, and you're making a hundred bucks. That's still not really rapping for money. But I'd rather do that than actually work at a restaurant, which I do, too. 'Cause you're promoting yourself. You can't just be a rapper and think that you're gonna put out a product in the stores and it's gonna sell. Shit doesn't work like that."

Treese wasn't waiting for someone to come along and give him a record deal or to recognize him at one of his shows and sign him up. There weren't even any major record labels in Chicago. He spoke with admiration about rap entrepreneurs like Jay-Z, who were building up capital, working hard to put out new products. "That's why I didn't put an album out and just have it sit there and know that I couldn't tour out of Chicago," Treese said. "What's the difference if I'm just doing local shows, getting a hundred dollars a show, two hundred dollars a show. It's a joke! You gotta be on the road, promoting your music, selling your music in other markets, and having your shit in stores."

"Well, I can respect that as an artist you gotta get paid," I said to Treese. "But I guess I always associated underground, independent rap with maintaining a conscious, anticapitalist stance, not with entrepreneurs calculating the best market strategy. And what kind of role model is Jay-Z, a hip hop powerhouse worth $550 million? I thought that being independent is about staying true to the art, rejecting the market."

But after years of doing restaurant work to make a living, Treese didn't share my poverty ethos. "Forget about Top Forty radio and forget about Best Buy. I'm not talking about that," Treese responded. "I'm talking about having your shit worldwide-distributed like Rawkus and Fat Beats was. If I wasn't doing that, what difference would it make if I had an album? Who's gonna know? Unless you got access to making hits, it's not even an option: Should I be major or should I be independent? You're independent 'cause you gotta be."

As much as I had hoped that underground rap could be the basis for an anticapitalist, anticorporate Hip Hop Nation, I realized that as an artist you had to make your life within the system. You could oppose the music industry and its distortion of the culture, but what other model was there in America besides the entrepreneurial one of self-reliance and self-promotion? It was just like the Hip Hop Revolución artists in Cuba who had to rely on state sponsorship to make a living. You made your music within, and despite, the constraints of each situation.

I was still curious as to whether I could make my music in Chicago as an Indian female emcee with an Australian accent. A mutual friend introduced me to Navraz—a feisty Punjabi American rapper and singer. She had grown up in the northern Chicago suburb of Plainsville and was a student at Loyola College. In a friend's home studio she sang for me the R&B-inflected chorus to her latest song. "Are you an exotic queen come up from my dreams / Are you my fantasy, right here to satisfy me? / Whatever, uh-uh fool, I am a woman like your mother." We clicked straight away, and before long we were writing and rehearsing songs together. We would mix in Punjabi bhanghra, a working-class Indian style that was popularized in the dance clubs in London.

Navraz and I performed with the local desi fusion band Funkadesi and the eclectic jazz guitarist Fareed Haque. Soon we were getting booked for Asian American nights at clubs and college campuses, Asian American charity dinners, and women's poetry festivals. I started moving in a self-enclosed world of Asian American rappers, spoken-word artists, and theater activists. The artists were mostly Asian Americans, and the audiences were mostly Asian American. It was yet another de facto segregated world that I came across in Chicago.

Many Asian Americans that I came across in this scene had grown up in predominantly white Chicago suburbs. They rapped about their experiences of racism while being raised in affluent white suburban enclaves. They were rebelling against the conformity of suburban life and their parents' expectations that they would become doctors or investment bankers. They justified their participation in the Hip Hop Nation by drawing on their experiences of racism in white society and marginality within their own communities.

For a while I enjoyed doing my music again, finding a place where it was accepted. But I didn't really relate to this scene. For a start, I wasn't Asian American. I had never really thought of myself as any kind of ethnic or hyphenated identity—Indian, desi, Asian. I didn't grow up in white suburbia, and I was raised among people of all different backgrounds—Filipinos, Chinese, Tongans, Aboriginals, Africans, as well as working-class whites. And when I performed in the US the songs that I had written in Australia—with references to local political events, people, and places—no one knew what I was talking about. At least when I performed in Cuba, nobody could understand what I was saying anyway.

The other problem was that the Asian American hip hop scene was completely divorced from the underground, where reputations were built through sheer hard work and mastery of lyrical wordplay. If you could get an audience hyped just by using the words *racism* and *oppression,* it wasn't really an educated hip hop audience.

There was a sense of social activism and commitment that I found appealing. At the same time I was uneasy with some of the terms that I heard used by Asian American artists— "brown liberation movement," "race consciousness," "Asian civil rights struggle." Some even called themselves black. But, as Anthony Kwame Harrison has argued, individuals' claims to hip hop legitimacy have to be grounded in their historical and political contexts.[15] Post-1965 waves of Asian emigration to the US were mostly from a professional class. If this generation of Asian Americans suffered racism, it was not generally the kind of institutional discrimination that prevents you from obtaining jobs and education, and keeps you in jail, on the streets, and on welfare. As recorded in the 2000 census, South Asians in particular had the highest average family income in the US. They were strongly upwardly mobile and financially successful. So what was the liberation they were after? How could the admittedly painful psychological effects of racist name-calling and social exclusion suffered by Asian Americans today possibly be compared with the Jim Crow laws that had disenfranchised African Americans, legally excluded them from white spaces, and denied them access to schools, housing, and jobs?

Like some white rappers, Asian American rappers could also rework hip hop as a vehicle to express their experiences of marginality and discrimination. But whether they could come together with blacks and Latinos in a broader hip hop culture depended on the existence of some shared ground. A minority of whites and Asian Americans who grew up alongside African Americans were able to gain entry into worlds like early underground hip hop. One example was the South Asian DJ Rekha, who grew up around mostly African Americans and second-generation Caribbean immigrants in Flushing and on Long Island in New York City.[16] But without those common lived experiences—or at least parallels in experience—the rhetoric of multiracial alliances and postures of Afro-Asian unity didn't have much resonance beyond small circles. And without shared social spaces and experiences, there was very little ground for multiracial political struggles. Underground rap couldn't bring people together across racial and ethnic lines unless there were existing alliances—and perhaps even a political movement— that had already brought them together.

The global Hip Hop Nation was fractured. As I traveled the globe, I saw more differences than similarities. And location mattered greatly in defining who you were. In Cuba I was a gringa, in Chicago I was an Australian, yet in Australia I was Indian. Growing up, people would ask me, "Where are you really from?" My exposure to the identity-saturated world of Asian Americans had taught me one thing. Much about who I was, the way I viewed the world, and my concerns as an artist came from my location in Australia. As I looked back, I realized that my experiences in the US were a world apart from my own initiation into hip hop in Australia and its cross-racial appeal at the time of a deepening antiracist political movement.

CHAPTER 3

Blackfulla Blackfulla

My odyssey around the globe had begun on Sydney's West Side in August 1995, when I saw the ad from Death Defying Theatre that announced a multimedia project with workshops in rapping, graffiti, and b-boying. Three months of workshops were to culminate in a large-scale performance known as Hip Hopera. After several years of full-time political activism in Sydney, I was starting to wonder why left-wing radicals and progressives were so confined to the downtown vegetarian-hippie-café-latte-drinking set while never reaching the vast working classes in the west of the city. The problem was that the left was culturally isolated. Its idea of a radical cultural night was lentil curries and folk songs on the guitar. Meanwhile, Aboriginal, Arabic, Pacific Islander, and white working-class youth out in western Sydney were embracing hip hop culture and becoming angry and inspired. I saw the Hip Hopera workshops as a way to connect with this nascent hip hop movement and to understand how hip hop might be the key to political expression and voice for a new generation of excluded youth.

Just as hip hop reached urban American minority populations in places like Chicago at a point of desperation after years of deindustrialization and urban decay, so the culture hit home for Aboriginal and immigrant youth in Australia at a time of intensifying poverty, unemployment, and despair. It was a generation that had grown up seeing marches in the streets, sit-ins, and community organizing. But now this generation faced a vacuum—of leadership, of politics, of direction. Could hip hop fill that void?

Aboriginal people in particular had a history of connecting to a Pan-African diaspora through music. When Bob Marley performed in Adelaide in 1979, his claim that "All Black men are brothers" was taken up as an anthem by indigenous people.[1] But could a black American form like hip hop still galvanize protest at a time when there was a dearth of political engagement? And could Marley's black men expand into Bambaataa's "Planet Rock" to incorporate the poor whites and immigrants who, along with Aboriginals, populated the fringes of the city? Despite Chicago's being a multiracial city, the segregation there made it harder to forge broader cross-racial alliances. In Sydney an unexpected turn of political events would bring us together across racial and ethnic lines, if briefly, in ways we hadn't thought possible before.

I kicked around the idea of going to the Hip Hopera workshops with my friend Waiata Telfer, a young Aboriginal woman who hailed from Adelaide. Could we be Australia's new Queen Latifah and MC Lyte? We had our doubts. With our braids and lack of vocal training, we felt more like Milli Vanilli.

I had met Waiata at a community theater workshop in the inner-city neighborhood of Newtown the year before. She was a slender woman with copper-colored skin and closely cropped hair. Although she had been pictured with loose wavy hair falling about her bare shoulders, I recognized her from the oversized billboard with the caption, "They say I'm too pretty to be an Aboriginal." The billboard, mounted above the main thoroughfare of Parramatta Road in inner-city Leichardt, was sponsored by the New South Wales Aboriginal Land Council's "Racism Sux" campaign.

As we strolled across to the park during a lunch break, Waiata explained, "The agent took that statement out of context when he used it for the ad. What I was saying was that I hated it when people said I was too pretty to be an Aboriginal. He took away the power of my words." When she went back to Adelaide,

Waiata's family was offended. "Think yer too pretty to be a black-fulla? Think yer too pretty to be one of us?" It prompted her to cut off all her hair.

Waiata grew up in public housing in a semirural town called Old Noarlunga, on the outskirts of Adelaide, with her mother and three brothers. Her mother came from Point Pearce Mission to the city to work as a domestic and later found work in a government program known as Aboriginal Hostels Ltd., which provided housing for Nungas—the term for Aboriginal people from the Southeast of South Australia who came to the city.[2]

When she was playing in the shallow streams and wide green paddocks of Old Noarlunga as a child, the people Waiata encountered were mostly Aboriginal. It was only when she went to primary school and started seeing predominantly white faces that she began to wonder, who am I? "*Yeah, you're an Abo.*" She had to go home and ask her mother what that meant. "My first year at primary school, I had a really clear memory that's when all the doors were closed, and that's when I started to get really angry," she related.

The rise of the Aboriginal land rights movement in the early 1970s forced Adelaide, like many other Australian cities at that time, to confront its troubled racist history. Hundreds of Aboriginal people were taking to the streets with megaphones and placards, occupying the main streets of the downtown area. As a child, Waiata accompanied her mother to packed community meetings where people were talking about native title, sovereignty, and the Gove Land Rights Case in which a Northern Territory judge upheld the legal doctrine of pre-British Australia as *terra nullius*, or "vacant land," that justified British settlement and the dispossession of Aboriginal people.

At school Waiata found that Aboriginal history was absent from textbooks about exploration and settlement of Australia. "They were telling me that Aboriginal people had died out. So it made me feel really angry and I said, 'Hey, hang on, this isn't true. What kind of history are you telling? It's bullshit!!! I'm Aboriginal and I'm alive, and this history book is saying that

I'm not.' And the teacher said to me, 'You're the student, I'm the teacher, and this is the true history because it's written.' "

So one day Waiata came to her history class dressed as a bush-ranger, complete with stocky black boots, a fake beard drawn on with a pen, and a wide-brimmed outback hat. Aboriginal bushrangers were outlaws and rebels during the late nineteenth century; Musquito, for example, was an escaped Aboriginal prisoner who ran raids against the white settlers from his vantage point in the bush and was sentenced to death by hanging. Waiata pointed two fingers at her teacher in mock imitation of a gun, and she told him that the history he was teaching wasn't true.

"I was really enraged that to me he was telling lies," she said. "I wanted to let him know, 'You don't know shit, all you're doing is reading out of a history book, and there's a lot of history here that you have missed.' I told him he should get books in there that told the truth. But at that time there were no books. The history books were written by the conquerors, and they said that Aboriginal people all died out with colds and smallpox." Waiata found herself sitting outside the principal's office and then suspended from all classes. She started cutting school; she had nothing to learn there anyway.

Every Sunday night in her preteen years, Waiata watched Molly Meldrum's *Countdown*, a sampling of local and inter-national music hits. Waiata lip-synched to Tina Turner and imitated Michael Jackson's dance steps. It was on *Countdown* that she first saw Bob Marley, and she begged her mother to take her to see him on his Survival Tour of Australia and New Zealand in 1979. Like many other young indigenous Australians, Waiata was drawn to Marley's Pan-Africanist invocations of black brotherhood.

Just a few years later it was rap that caught her attention on the same show. "When I saw Grandmaster Flash and Melle Mel with "The Message," I was in grade six or seven, and I was really blown away," recalls Waiata. "I just went '*Shit!*' One was for the rhyming, I'd never seen that or heard that before. And, two, for what he was saying. It hit home, really political stuff coming from another person who was black." Aboriginal people in South Australia didn't live in ghettos as such; they were dispersed into white society. But the song resonated.

Along with the music, Waiata was captivated by b-boy culture. She and her little brother would watch *Breakdance*, *Beat Street*, and *Electric Boogaloo* on an old Betamax machine, and they'd try to copy the moves. When she was thirteen, Waiata had a dance crew with her little brother and another boy, and they carried their cardboard strip everywhere they went.

"I used to spin on my back and do 'the worm,'" she remembered. "As usual, the boys used to do all the power moves. My brother would do the windmills, and I'd be there doing the moonwalk and the robot. I remember I wanted to be just like Baby Love from the Rock Steady Crew, '*b-b-boys and b-b-girls, all around the world*.' It was about sharing a message and also having some fun, dancing and having a good time. I'd grown up in a household where there was just a lot of violence and exposure to criminal activity because of poverty," she said. "So for me music was a way to escape, really, and have a sense of happiness. 'Cause the life I was growing up in had some pretty hard elements."

Waiata left school at sixteen and went to Sydney to perform with the Aboriginal Dance Theatre, but she sustained a neck injury during a rehearsal. At the time I met her, she was wearing a neck brace, taking painkillers to stave off the frequent headaches, and working as a commercial model to make ends meet until her workers' compensation came through. After we met at the Newtown workshop, Waiata and I began to work as facilitators, doing theater workshops with young Aboriginal and migrant kids.

A week after I saw the ad from Death Defying Theatre, Waiata and I made the trek out to Sydney's west, a sprawling area on the periphery of the city populated by Lebanese, Vietnamese, Chinese, and Pacific Islander immigrants and whites. Worlds away from the tourist brochure images of golden sand beaches and the silhouette of the Sydney Opera House and Harbour Bridge, the west is the massive underbelly of the city. Nestled in the basin of the Cumberland Plain, prefabricated fibro houses—made of asbestos and cement board—and low-income public housing estates stretch sixty miles west to the Blue Mountains range. In the postwar period significant numbers of European immigrants were drawn to the southwestern region to work as unskilled laborers in industrial areas such as the Minto industrial estate or in construction.

Up until the 1970s, there was a "White Australia" policy in place that restricted non-white immigrants from entering the country. After this policy was officially repealed with the passage of the Racial Discrimination Act in 1975, there was a significant rise in nonwhite immigration. Whole villages and small towns from Lebanon were transplanted to areas like Lakemba and Bankstown after 1975, during the Lebanese civil war. Asian immigration also increased dramatically, with places like Cabramatta, a southwestern suburb of Sydney, becoming a hub for Vietnamese settlement. Many of these immigrants filled the growing need for unskilled labor on assembly lines. But as in other Western capitalist countries around the globe, manufacturing went into decline during the 1980s as factories relocated overseas and cheap imports replaced local production. Unemployment among Lebanese youth rose to 43 percent by the early 1990s.[3] Many parts of the west began to experience high rates of unemployment, poverty, and crime, as they were increasingly cut off from the prosperity of the gentrifying inner city and the mostly white north of the city. Immigrant communities in western Sydney were demonized with talk of "Asian crime waves," "Asian invasion," and "ethnic gangs."

With internal and external migration the racial makeup of Sydney's west had changed dramatically. The earlier denigrating stereotype of the "westie" referred to white working-class youth with mullet haircuts, Ugg boots, and checked flannel shirts who lived in western Sydney. In contrast, the post–White Australia westie rocked the latest fly gear—Adidas track pants, Nikes, and Fila hoodies. And in true hip hop style, b-boys, graffiti writers, and emcees reclaimed the term *westie* and redefined it as "West Side."

The Death Defying Theatre workshops were being held in the recreation facility of the Bankstown Multicultural Youth Center. Waiata and I took the Strathfield-Bankstown train out to Bankstown station and got off at the Old Town Plaza. Side by side were a Lebanese beauty salon; a Chinese herb center; a travel agent advertising cheap fares to Beirut, Jordan, Damascus, and Amman; and a Vietnamese butcher selling pig feet, cow feet, and pork neck. Two burka-clad Muslim girls were talking animatedly on the corner. On the opposite corner was a Maori man in a tank top with traditional tattoos on his face, arms, and legs. A group of elderly Vietnamese men played mahjong on a table in the plaza. They were all oblivious to the white guy on a megaphone outside the Bag-A-Bargain who belted out the discounts to be found in the store in a broad Aussie accent. We walked down a few streets to the youth center.

Khaled Sabsabi, aka Peacefender, was a serious young Lebanese-Australian man whose brown eyes peered out from behind dark locks of curly hair. Standing in his Nikes, hooded sweatshirt, and blue jeans, he shuffled papers on a desk in front of a rowdy roomful of adolescent Lebanese boys in the youth center. The boys, fourteen and fifteen years old, sat with growing limbs squeezed into small wooden desks. They wore Adidas trackies, Pumas, and Nikes; some sported bandannas and baseball caps; and others had their hair gelled back. As Waiata and I entered the room, a sea of eyes turned toward us.

"Um, we're looking for the rap workshops by Death Defying Theatre?" I mumbled to nobody in particular.

There was silence. I studied my fingernail. Khaled didn't look up from his papers. After what seemed like a very long time, the boys turned their attention back to their noisy conversations. One pair started to wrestle in the corner.

I looked over at Waiata, and we exchanged desperate glances that said, "*What are we doing here*?" I turned and walked quickly out of the room, followed closely by Waiata. Outside, in the warm spring air of early September, we shook our heads and sighed. We were too old for this—I was twenty-one and Waiata was twenty-four. Khaled trudged out soon after, his shoulders hunched over and his hands dug deep into his pockets. "Hey, listen," he said, encouragingly, "this here is more of an after-school activity for some kids of the community. But next week we're starting to work with young people out at Casula Power-house, if you wanna come out there instead."

To get to Casula we caught the South Line train from Central Station, passing the Granville, Fairfield, Liverpool, and Cambelltown stations. At the stops we saw school kids in their uniforms with bulky backpacks, some of them standing in circles and rhyming or b-boying. As the train whooshed in and out of pitch-dark tunnels, extended landscapes of graffiti pieces were visible along the concrete walls facing the tracks. Bombers played a game of cat-and-mouse with the transit police, tagging ten places for every piece that the "transits" destroyed. There was graffiti on the steel platform supports, across the sides of houses—one piece of graffiti even graced the base of a lone gum tree. At one section of the tracks was a state-commissioned "Australiana" mural. Angry scrawls of silver tags contemptu-ously covered the beatific scenes of the Harbour Bridge, beaches, koalas, and kangaroos.

Just a few dozen feet from the Georges River in the south-western suburb of Liverpool—once a key manufacturing hub—the imposing structure of the Casula Powerhouse loomed large against the gray-blue sky. A former power plant, the Casula Powerhouse was a newly refurbished public arts center, complete with galleries and large open performance spaces. The long concrete cylindrical cooling towers framing the building were a quaint reminder of the industrial past. The whole con-struction—testament to the new priorities of investor-driven arts councils—stood in stark contrast to the decay of the dein-dustrialized landscape and the vast surrounding public housing estates created during the 1960s urban renewal schemes that relocated low-income families from the inner-city slums to places like Liverpool.

On the lawns of the Casula Powerhouse, twenty-three-year-old Sharline Bezzina, aka Spice, a graffiti artist and an arts worker of Maltese descent, had laid heavy-duty canvas sheets out on the grass. Kids with spray cans painted pieces in stylized block designs. Even on the inoffensive precut canvas, the letters careened off the page and assaulted the observer with hard-edged three-dimensional outlines and fill-ins of red, blue, and yellow fading to white. They sat uneasily on the manicured lawns of a former industrial power plant.

Waiata and I wandered past several open gallery spaces. We paused when we came to the central amphitheater that had been converted from a boiler room. We were in awe of the airy spaciousness, the squeaky laminate floors, and the metal beams high overhead. Following the tones of a sampled drum loop, we cautiously approached what looked like an enormous dressing room. In preparation for the first workshop, Khaled had set up an Ensoniq EPS sampling keyboard, a four-track cassette tape recorder, a microphone, and turntables along several trestle tables joined lengthwise. Khaled was one of the Australian pioneers of the idea of hip hop workshops as part of a community arts model to bring together people of different backgrounds in support of social change. His own group, COD (Course of Destruction), united Lebanese and Turkish rappers from Auburn at a time when there was significant tension between these ethnic groups. Their shows were attended by young people from both communities, creating new lines of solidarity and connection. After remixing a show soundtrack for Death Defying Theatre in the late 1980s, Khaled proposed the idea of the theater's doing a big media event focusing on hip hop, using the idea of opera to emphasize the grand scale of the event. The idea was funded, and Khaled—along with Morgan Lewis, event director, and several other arts workers—worked to make their vision a reality.

Khaled was going through vinyl records in some crates to the side. He selected a record and put it on the turntable, manipulating it with one hand. Girls and boys of different ages and ethnicities milled around the room. Some watched Khaled with a timid curiosity and others hung back, whispering to each other.

Just then, two young men swaggered to the front of the room, where a few microphones were set up on tall stands. One of them, a Lebanese guy, wearing baggy jeans and a bandanna across his head, grabbed a mic and starting rapping into it, even though it was not connected. "One-two, one-two," he repeated pointlessly, mimicking a sound check. "Yo, my niggaz in da house, I'm tha mutha-fuckin' gangsta," he rapped in an American accent. The other guy pulled his baseball cap to one side and took the other mic. "I don't like fake hoes, so all you bitches in the house take note." "Oh, yeah," responded the Lebanese guy, two extended fingers gesturing from a bent arm close to his body. They turned to each other and bumped shoulders in a congratulatory hug.

Khaled had still not looked up from his drum machine, and for a few minutes, while the wannabe gangstas bounced around on the makeshift stage, he appeared to be concentrating intensely on his task. Then he turned off the drum machine and fixed his eyes on the Lebanese kid.

"Do you have a sister?" asked Khaled.

"Um, yes."

"Do you have a mother?"

"Yes," the Lebanese kid answered slowly, not sure where this was going.

"Are they bitches?"

"Nah," the Lebanese kid scowled, "'course not."

"Every woman is someone's sister or mother or daughter. If we're doing hip hop here in Australia, it can't be about imitating what you hear on the radio or see in the music videos. It has to be about your experiences and the issues facing your communities."

"Yeah, alright," nodded the Lebanese kid, chastened. "I feel you, nigga."

Munkimuk, an Aboriginal hip hop producer and founder of the crew South West Syndicate (SWS), was walking along the Hume Highway with a few of his boys when a beat-up Honda pulled up alongside them, and Khaled stuck his head out of the window.

"Brothers, I got something for you, man."

"Yeah, whaddya want, bro?"

"There's this hip hop gig. It's got, like, all of Sydney and Melbourne hip hop–type people. Are you guys in or what?"

"Yeah, we'll throw something together, no worries."

SWS was a self-described "criminal associate" rap group whose turf stretched from the whole Bankstown area down to Canterbury, all the way back to Liverpool, with connections in Redfern. There were thirty-odd members of SWS—Aboriginal, Pacific Islander, Lebanese, and white. The key Aboriginal members of the group—including Brothablack, Munkimuk, Dax, and Naz—had moved to the Bankstown-Punchbowl area with their families through the Housing for Aborigines relocation scheme in the 1970s. Relocated families often lacked the networks of support that they had in the inner city, as well as community centers, public transportation, and other amenities. Brothablack, Munkimuk, Dax, and Naz were from some of the first Aboriginal families to move to the area, and they all lived along the same bus line. They found in hip hop a way of building community in the new environment of Sydney's west.

Among the Lebanese members of SWS was Mohammed, a young man who had been shot in the neck and was in a wheelchair. "We're all coming up in the same social, economic situation out west—Lebanese, Aboriginal, whites," said Munkimuk, "that's why we came together through hip hop culture."

Munkimuk, dubbed the godfather of Aboriginal hip hop, was twenty-seven, a lanky, light-skinned Koori. He began producing in the 1980s with a four-track tape recorder, a guitar, a keyboard, and a mic. The record button on the four-track was broken, so he had to sit with one finger pressed down on the button in order to record. "I had to figure out, how do you put this stuff together? No one told me," he said. "It was all trial and error, pulling apart tracks and figuring out, hold on—there's, like, a bass line, and a guitar part, keyboard part, singing. How does it all work? I taught myself guitar, keyboards, and then started figuring out how to put it together. When I started out, I didn't sample at all; it was all my original compositions. I would listen to a lot of old funk records, listen to the Bootsy Collins bass lines, and then work out how to play like that. Then, in 1994, I got loans from Mohammed and from my brother, who was working full time at the scrap metal yard, to buy a sequencer and a Roland DJ70 sampler. It had a scratch pad, so that I could do the cuts on the scratch pad."

For Munkimuk it all started in 1984 with *Beat Street*. "Jiggin' school, getting some money, and going and watchin' *Beat Street* every day, 'cause I wanted to see how they did those windmills and all those mad moves," he said. "First time you saw it, it was like, 'Whoa, wait a second, I want to do that, man. That looks pretty cool.' So next day I'm back at the cinema again. Next day I'm back there again. It's like a religion, going there every day to watch *Beat Street*." He and some friends started going to inner-city Redfern, a densely populated Aboriginal enclave where some of the local kids were b-boying. Later they also joined a local graffiti crew from Redfern called Black Connection. From b-boying and graffiti, Munkimuk began rapping, and he created SWS in 1992. "I wasn't that interested in school," he said. "For English class I was in the English-as-a-Second-Language group, when English was my first language. The only class that I ever did good in was art, so I hardly ever bothered to turn up to school. The people in our crew were not really school goers. So we started hanging out, and the hip hop evolved from that. It broke the boredom."

Shannon Williams, aka Brothablack, was fourteen when he joined SWS a few years later. Brothablack, a tall Murri, was listening to hip hop—Big Mike from the Geto Boys, Run-DMC, Public Enemy, NWA—rapping over the top of it and then coming up with his own rhymes. One day he and his older brother went over to Munkimuk's place, and Munkimuk gave Shannon four lines to rap in a song called "The Syndicate." He kept going back and soon became part of the crew. At that time Munkimuk's small apartment, on Harcourt Street in East Hills, was a hub for hip hop.

"Back in those days there wasn't too many outlets for us to turn to for hip hop or for self-expression," recalled Brothablack.

"We had to make our own little communities." Munkimuk was the conductor of the whole operation. He would write rhymes and direct the ensemble, thinking about which kind of raps would bring out the strengths of each member. The group was more than a rap crew; it was an extended family—the members knew each others' parents, brothers, and sisters, and their mothers even used to catch the bus together.

For young people out in western Sydney, hip hop was a means of survival. "We're not doin' it to piss our parents off. We're not tryin' to fit into a scene," Brothablack told a reporter from Radio National. "Hip hop is our life and it's what we do. We're rapping for our lives."

"If it wasn't for hip hop, most of the members of our crew'd be in jail," added Munkimuk.[4]

Munkimuk and Brothablack weren't the only ones who credited hip hop with keeping them away from crime and drugs. At seventeen the Aboriginal rapper Chris Amtuani was in the Minda Juvenile Justice Center and charged with armed robbery. He says he had been holding up stores since he was fifteen, and one day his shit was outta luck. Khaled and another arts worker, Vahid Vahed, made trips out to the Minda JJ to produce a song by Amtuani. Amtuani's song portrayed the bleak world of the lockup where, he said, he was "writing rhymes to stay alive."

Deejaying, b-boying, and graffiti writing drew on a language of sound, bodily movement, and images that could move relatively easily across regional and racial boundaries. Rapping was not so universal. Munkimuk recounted the time he met with the rap legend Ice-T on his Sydney tour. Munkimuk escorted Ice-T to a few local events and at one there was an Australian rapper who was rapping in an American accent. Ice-T wanted to take on the guy because he thought that he was making fun of them. Munkimuk had to explain to Ice-T that it wasn't a parody. American rap was the only variety available at the time; there were no other models.

Why was it that, as we tried to rap, the words came out in American accents? Because rapping in an Australian accent sounded ridiculous. For example, in the phrase, "You don't stop," Americans draw the vowel out to sound like *staaap,* in contrast to the short, clipped *stop* of an Aussie accent. We all admired the smooth lyrical style of Baba Israel, a white emcee at the Death Defying Theatre workshops who had grown up in Brooklyn with an Australian mother and an American father. While most of us had old-school flow, rapping in basic rhymes that fell on the beat, Baba was already taking it to another level, with complex and layered raps.

But others had a different explanation. "If all we ever listen to is American rap, how are we supposed to rap in our own accents?" asked Sahar Ekermawi, aka Dr. Nogood, of the all-female Lebanese trio Notorious Sistaz and Dr. Nogood. Dr. Nogood was a fresh-faced young woman with a deep voice; her father was from Jerusalem and her mother was Palestinian, born in Lebanon.

"It just doesn't sound right, rapping in an Aussie accent," countered Natalie Serman, one of the Notorious Sistaz, alluding to white Australian underground rap groups from Sydney's west like Def Wish Cast. The latter had pioneered a style of rhyming in the truncated and guttural bursts of a broad working-class Aussie accent. "That doesn't fit the way that most of us here speak, either."

"Well, how do you guys talk then?" asked Khaled.

"I guess that most of us didn't speak English till we came to Australia," replied Natalie. "And we speak mostly Arabic at home. At school they say we have a 'wog' accent and we have to learn to speak right. But this is how we speak."[5]

"Then why don't you introduce some Arabic into your rapping?" suggested Khaled. "If language is about who you are, then English is only half of you, right?

The next week the Notorious Sistaz and Dr. Nogood came to the workshop, proud of the new rhyme they'd come up with. "You don't have to stand on the corner and slang / 'cause you got your own thang / We're gonna zig-zag you in a way you never knew / Smile *ma-shi* [walking] and feel the *junoon* [madness]," rapped Nirvana, one of the Notorious Sistaz, to applause and whistles from everyone in the workshop.

Khaled was a storyteller. He was born in the northern Lebanese city of Tripoli, but his family was forced to flee in 1978 during the civil war, and they came to live in western Sydney. Khaled tried to fit in, but he couldn't relate to the staples of Aussie culture—cricket, pubs, and rock music. From the early days, when he listened to hip hop on the national youth radio station 2JJ's black music night, Khaled was transfixed by the technologies of sampling and break beats. The reception of 2JJ—which broadcast through the emergency low-power transmitter from the ABC (Australian Broadcasting Corporation) tower at Gore Hill—was erratic in the northern and eastern suburbs but somewhat better in the western ones, especially at night. Tuning in to the AM dial at 1540 kHz, Khaled recorded the songs on cassette. These tapes would be copied and recopied, passed from hand to hand, the dull and static-ridden sounds a shadow of their former vitality but nevertheless treated as artifacts from a faraway civilization.

Along with a number of other kids in his neighborhood, Khaled started out by rhyming. But they had no one to make beats for them. So he turned his parents' garage into a music studio, making beats with basic analog methods like direct drive turntables or cutting tape. Khaled's first piece of equipment was

© Ian Hobbs

Khaled Sabsabi

a four-track tape recorder that allowed him to record four tracks on a quarter-inch cassette by combining sides A and B and splitting the left and right channels. He found the break beat that he wanted to use, recorded it on track one, and looped it by manually inserting it over and over. Then he rewound the tape and played track one while recording another sample on track two. He worked with the precision of a surgeon, manually quantizing tracks one and two in order to maintain a coherence in the overall tempo and rhythm. He would repeat the procedure for track three. Once the three tracks were completed, they were combined on track four. For a three-bar sample of six seconds, he needed to loop it thirty times on each track to have a three-minute beat. A one-bar sample of two seconds would need to be looped ninety times. It took almost a week to lay down a three-minute beat.

Like DJs and producers everywhere, Khaled was obsessed with "digging in the crates"—searching for vinyl records—and always on the lookout for the hottest break beats in the most unexpected places. He started out using his dad's record collection of disco and Arabic music. Then Khaled borrowed records from his circle of Arab friends in western Sydney and also began to frequent a store called Disco City, which specialized in funk and early hip hop. At this time the shift was taking place from analog to digital, so people were throwing out entire collections of records. "There were secondhand record shops, like Ashwood's on Pitt Street and mission-run stores like the Salvation Army, where I spent many hours and days going through thousands of records," said Khaled. "I limited myself to not spending more than two dollars per record." Over the years he accumulated a collection of more than seven thousand records.

As a producer, Khaled recognized the power of sound to narrate a life shaped by war, displacement, and exile. Like many other Lebanese youth, he had grown up in the shadow of the fifteen-year civil war in Lebanon that began in 1975 with hostilities between the Palestinian Liberation Organization, Lebanese political parties, and Lebanese Muslim and Christian militias backed by Syria and Israel. As tensions between Israel and the resistance mounted, Israel invaded southern Lebanon in 1978 and again in 1982, causing massive casualties and an exodus that saw many Lebanese flee to Australia. Khaled began to incorporate the derbukka drums and the melodic buzuq into beats, meshing the sonic landscapes of his childhood with the hardcore pulse of the urban periphery.

At the time of Hip Hopera, Khaled was living with his parents in their home in Auburn, on the West Side. His hundreds of crates were scattered throughout the garage and bedroom, stacked in no apparent order but cataloged meticulously in his head. He could find the desired break beat or record in a matter of minutes. It was there that I first witnessed the magic of making a track, as Khaled put down beats for a song that Waiata had written, "Fuck the Brady Bunch." Khaled imported a simple, sparse drum sample into the thick plastic gray EPS and looped it, then he added a funky bass line. Rummaging through one crate he came up with a well-worn album, *Super Bad* by Terminator X of Public Enemy. From one of the tracks he extracted Sister Souljah's battle cry, "We are at war," adding it at the beginning of the beat and then again at the end. More samples were diced up, rearranged, looped, and then added to the beat, along with screaming horns and lightning shots of cymbal. The result was an explosive sonic amalgam that extended Chuck D's proverbial black planet to a blackfulla pondering her life on an Adelaide street corner.

As we continued with the workshops, it became apparent to me that hip hop was thriving on the West Side because these young people had something to say and hip hop culture was the vehicle through which they had chosen to say it. I had also wanted to rap because I felt that I had so much to say, and I too wanted to be heard. I was heavily involved in campaigning around issues from East Timor's right to independence and a woman's right to choose to Aboriginal deaths in police custody. Just as rap music had inspired me to political awareness, so I wanted to use it to talk about social issues. The song that I wrote for Hip Hopera was a political tract criticizing the Australian government's program of nuclear testing in the Pacific. It was more like a master's thesis than a rap song. I was making one mistake. Just like when I was an activist, I was talking at my audience rather than talking to them. My rap icons, like KRS-One and Public Enemy, may have had a political agenda, but above all they were artful lyricists who knew how to move a crowd. Young hip hop audiences didn't wanted to be preached to; they wanted to hear someone give voice to their experiences, and they wanted it to be funky.

But how could *I* give voice to the experiences of these young people? I didn't have a personal connection to the issues I was writing about in the same way that the others did. For all my outrage at black deaths in police custody, I had never lost a friend or a relative to the criminal justice system or been brought up in an environment that made jail one of the only options. Part of me was afraid that all my third-person political rhetoric was just a cover for really having nothing to say.

After three months of workshops, beat making, and practicing our rhymes, in late November we were finally ready to take to the stage in our rehearsals for the upcoming Hip Hopera concert. It was chaotic as groups tried to memorize their lyrics, schedule sessions with Khaled to finish their beats, and then practice with their beats.

There was an uncomfortable silence in the auditorium of the Casula Powerhouse when two young belly dancers came on stage. Heavily made up, with thick mascara and glitter on their eyelids, the young women wore revealing gold-sequined halter tops with tassels and matching bikini briefs. They came out demurely, shielded behind face veils, gyrating their hips to a prerecorded beledi rhythm. Then the beat kicked in, and they cast off the veils as the belly dance morphed into a sexually suggestive funk dance. A few young men from the audience whooped in appreciation.

Enter Mohammed W.O.G., a Lebanese-Australian rapper from Auburn. "I'm worshipped so give me respect when I'm on stage," rapped Mohammed, who wore a chain with a cross studded with fake diamonds, and shiny Adidas trackies. "I never neglect my rhymes since a very young age." The belly dancers sandwiched themselves on either side of him, grinding their hips together with his. Then they turned their backs to the audience, hands on their knees while shaking their booty in the air. The rap continued: "Every time I turn around I see another brother dead / Either he gets stabbed or shot up in the head." As he clutched at his crotch, Mohammed repeated the chorus of the song over and over: "Another brother dead, another brother dead." As the spectacle unfolded on stage, the implications were unsettling. Despite the hope many of us had placed in rap as a political voice for disenfranchised youth, this was the other reality of rap as a commodity that objectified women and glorified conspicuous consumption and gratuitous violence. The American hip hop writer Yvonne Bynoe said that the globalization of hip hop divorced the culture from black American history. The global culture industries promoted stereotypes about black criminality and violence, turned blackness into a fad to be consumed, and exported cultural identities rather than allowing youth to create their own.[6] Looking back on the experience, there seemed to be some truth to what Bynoe was saying. For every Brothablack or Khaled, how many Mohammed W.O.G.s were out there, consuming and imitating unrealistic images of African Americans that widened the cultural divide even further? It was impossible to know, but one could only guess.

The performance at Casula in front of an audience of five hundred people began with a freestyle with all the performers on the stage. Cyphers opened up on the floor. The backdrop was an immense canvas of shadow-style graffiti. Morganics, Elf Transporter, and Baba—members of the hip hop crew MetaBass 'n' Breath—started up a human beatbox.

Young men jostled, gestured, and shoved each other on the small stage in a show of bravado. After a succession of male rappers took the mic, Nirvana, Dr. Nogood, and the Fijian-Tongan rapper Danielle Tuwai made their way to the front and started up a chant: "All the ladies in the house say, 'Hip Hop rocks.'" Then Waiata took the mic and sang in a bluesy, soulful voice, "Aborigines must be free, to control their destiny," and the beatbox slowed to a deep pulse. "Maybe if I was white, living would be alright, but how can I live in a white world, when my spirit is black." The room went silent. "This goes out to all the Aboriginal people in the audience," she said, raising her right arm. "This was and will always remain Aboriginal land."

Suddenly, there was commotion in the back of the room. The audience parted as a red car appeared and then inched its way to the front. Accompanied by a funk bass line with some horns, the members of SWS leaped from the car and settled across the stage. "Mr. Speaker, there seems to be an intervention," rapped Munkimuk. "Fire'n a couple of shots to get attention / We're doin' a home invasion on parliament house / We're throwing them overpaid politicians out." In between, they sampled the P-funk mantra: "If you ain't gonna get it on, then take your dead ass home." On stage was Brothablack's four-year-old baby cousin, who joined them in a squeaky voice. Brothablack came forward. "Got brothas like me behind bars and in the gutter / Portraying us as stupid black fuckers / The white man's plan is getting outta hand / We're being hung up in your cells across the land."

Next up was Ebony Williams, a fifteen-year-old Aboriginal girl of Wiradjuri descent from inner-city Newtown. Ebony and Danielle Tuwai appeared together as Two Indij. "This one's dedicated to my mother. I love you," said Ebony. The beat kicked in, and she rapped, "As I look at what I've become / I've listened to my father / Tryin' to run my life from one place to another / I listen and I think / He doesn't really know / For god's sake, he's never seen me before." Danielle sang on the R&B-inflected chorus, "You never seem to understand me, you never know how much you mean to me." She finished up by saying, "I'd like to dedicate this to the woman who's been there my whole life since day one. She's been my mother and my father." Danielle had never met her Maori father, just as Ebony had never met her African American father. The song was a letter to the absent fathers of their generation and a tribute to the mothers who raised them alone.

The stage was lit up briefly by a strobe light, and then two b-boys entered. In one corner there were turntables set up, and DJ ASK was spinning "Jam on It," by Newcleus. In a twenty-second segment, the b-boys began with measured footwork around the perimeter of the circle, then spun on the floor, and finally dropped into a freeze, legs in splits and facing each other.

The next set was Notorious Sistaz and Dr. Nogood in camouflage fatigues. Video footage of soldiers flashed on the screen behind them as they performed a military routine reminiscent of Public Enemy's S1W. "This is for the Gs, and this is for the hustlers," sang Natalie. "Smoke that fat sack, while we're singin' this to ya." An image of a moving target filled the screen, followed by a red-tipped missile flying through the air.

A frenzied, hard-core beat kicked in, and Dr. Nogood began to rap in her deep voice: "Notorious Sistaz and Dr. Nogood / Bringing on the beat with a real attitude / Notorious Sistaz everyday, I say / Getting their men from around the way." Dr. Nogood pointed the mic down toward her mouth. She sported a baseball cap on backward that read Dr. Nogood.

The audience at the rehearsal broke out in cheers and whistles. "Sistas with flava / They'll cut you like a razor," Dr. Nogood continued, crouching at the front of the stage while images flashed on the screen above of soldiers hiding behind a building as explosions from mortars and shells pounded the earth in front of them. "So don't think of pulling any shit with them / 'Cause they're the sisters from above the rim."

As they rapped, the Notorious Sistaz and Dr. Nogood began a call-and-response sequence with the hyped-up audience. "Just kickin' the flow so so, yippedy yo," rapped Dr. Nogood, and the audience chanted back, "Go sistas, go sistas, No good, No good." Nirvana strode across the stage in her combat boots, and with heads nodding all around she rapped, "In the 'hood looking yella as we kick it to the fellas / Punk, you better recognize!"

Waiata and I were waiting in the wings, and we locked hands briefly before jumping on the stage. "We are at war," declared Sista Souljah on the sample. "I turn the channels over in my

Waiata and the author at Hip Hopera, November 1995

head," began Waiata, "and there I meet the nightmare." The beat kicked in. "My mum's bleeding, she's nearly half dying / Alice cooks a stew and the dishes need drying / I woke up with bruises, couldn't walk to school / Marcia gets a boyfriend and my classmates think it's cool." "The Brady Bunch, the Brady Bunch," we chanted on the chorus, "I wanna see a black face. The Brady Bunch, this the way we say fuck the Brady Bunch." The room resounded as people chanted on the last line with us. For a multiracial generation that was force-fed the saccharine images of white suburban American paradise, it was a moment of catharsis.

Many aspiring rappers launched their careers at the Casula show; others said what they had to say and then moved on to other things. Looking back on the basic old-school rhymes, the hard-core beats, and the simple raw truth in the lyrics, it might be easy to dismiss the scene as one of youthful idealism. But it was also a unique place, where multiple histories and landscapes converged through the black American form of hip hop, where the pain and horror of forced Palestinian exile mirrored Aboriginal displacement and genocide. It was a moment before the Australian music industry started promoting mostly white male

Waiata performing at Hip Hopera, November 1995

rappers, when women felt empowered to take to the mic. And it was a statement by an excluded generation that did not feel represented by politicians or by the media it consumed. But could this translate into a political movement?

The show ended with another freestyle session, everyone up on stage, including Khaled. The eleven-year-old Lebanese rapper Mega D from The Three Little Shits rhymed, "Yo, I decapitate the mic with my skills ya know / I can't wait till the next one tries to step to me / Can he really compete with the lyrical dictionary / At first glance, ya may say that I'm a criminal / 'Cause of my baggy pants and my shirt that's original." He closed out his rhyme with "Now I gotta go, it's past my bedtime."

In the period after Hip Hopera, I moved to Redfern, the inner-city neighborhood that was home to a large majority of Sydney's Aboriginal population. Bordered by a commuter railway station to the west and stretching to the busy thoroughfare of Elizabeth Street to the east, Redfern was a collection of narrow streets with Victorian two-story terrace houses. It was only a few miles from the central business district, and developers had begun to take an interest in available properties.

Redfern had historically been the site of a local black power movement, as young Kooris moving to the city en masse during the sixties in search of work began to hear about the Black Panthers, the Indians' occupation of Alcatraz, and decolonization movements in Africa. Rural migrants came from the north coast and western part of the state, and included Wiradjuri groups from central New South Wales.

Regent Street—with its famous pub the Empress Hotel—was a hive of activity. Inspired by the community service work of the Black Panthers and faced with growing police abuse and harassment in the neighborhood, a group of Koori activists set up a legal services center on Regent Street in 1970, and a year later they started a free medical clinic. In the early seventies a group of Aboriginal writers and actors set up the Black Theatre in a warehouse on Regent Street, and their first activity involved street theater during a land rights demonstration. In the eighties Koori activists started Radio Redfern in a small house on Cope Street, broadcasting under the license of another station. In 1993 Radio Redfern was converted into Koori Radio.

During the mid- to late 1990s Redfern was undergoing a cultural renaissance of sorts. Koori artists held exhibitions in the empty warehouses along Redfern Street. In 1995 the American rapper Ice Cube visited Redfern to launch Koori Radio, and from then on it saw a constant stream of Aboriginal artists, activists, and musicians.

Spanning the length of the wall facing the Redfern train station was a mural by local Kooris that narrated the story of their journey to the present. "40,000 years is a long, long time … 40,000 years still on my mind," the mural began, referring to the known period that Aboriginal people had occupied the country. There was a symbol of a ship with several tall masts, representing the First Fleet—the ships that came from Britain in 1788 to set up the colony. Here there was a thick black line down the center of the mural, marking a moment of rupture in the indigenous experience. Juxtaposed with a bush scene of gum trees and a naked Aboriginal boy standing before a Christian mission was a boomerang flying over a series of urban rooftops. There

Redfern mural

Redfern mural

© Samantha Lazzaro

was the profile of an Aboriginal woman dressed as a domestic, with a look of mourning, black and yellow rays radiating out from her. On the opposite wall was a mural that read, "Say Know to Drugs: For The Next Generation." It contained a black figure behind bars, with handcuffs painted in the surrounding border and the caption "Law and Order." Next to it, an image of a curled snake creating a yin-yang type of symbol separated a figure sitting alone in a corner from a circle of hands showing "unity."

Adjoining the mural was Eveleigh Street—a section of row houses referred to as "the Block." It was handed over to a self-organized collective of Aboriginal people known as the Aboriginal Housing Corporation in 1973, after a battle with local residents and landlords. It was one of the first experiments in Aboriginal-managed housing, breaking down fences to create shared living spaces.[7] Kooris migrating to the city saw the Block as a spiritual Mecca, an opportunity for affordable housing, and a way to retain kinship with other Kooris in the alien big city.

At the entrance to the Block, an Aboriginal flag flew from a flagpole, signaling that you were entering Aboriginal territory. There was an enormous mural of the Aboriginal flag painted on the side of a building: half black to represent Aboriginal people, half red for the crimson-brown soil of the land, and a yellow sun, the giver of life, in the center. The narrow houses with their wrought-iron balconies were set amid eucalyptus and tufts of overgrown grass, the skyscrapers of Sydney's downtown area visible in the background. There would be kids jumping rope in the street, teenagers sitting on stoops with boom boxes, older people outside relaxing in the shade, and, on occasion, people gathered around fires on the pavement at night. While in town to give concerts, visiting US rap artists such as Chuck D, The Fugees, and Michael Franti all have spent time at the Block.

At the same time police cars were permanently stationed at the entrance to Eveleigh Street and would make random incursions into the Block. White drug users from Newtown could be found shooting up in the alleyways or in search of the cheap drugs sold by Aboriginal children. When I once went to the local police station to report a bag of mine had been stolen, I walked out in disgust at the racist questioning of the police: "Did you see who it was? Was it a fuckin' Abo?"

Awakened by shouts in the early hours of the morning, I would look out from my window onto the back alley at brutal acts of violence, sometimes a taxi driver or hapless drunk being robbed for cash, sometimes only the black leather jacket of an officer visible as he pummeled his fists into a black kid. Every two weeks I would visit the Redfern social security office to collect my unemployment benefits, or "the dole," since I was trying to finish my degree part time. A room full of jobless brown and black people stared blankly at a booming television set as they waited to be called to a social worker to describe their employment-seeking efforts and then pick up a check for $120.

It was at this time that the specter of white supremacy raised its head yet again in the form of a red-headed, blue-eyed owner of a fish-and-chips shop who hailed from the northern Queensland town of Ipswich. Pauline Hanson ran for a seat in Australia's House of Representatives in March 1996. After publicly criticizing welfare benefits for Aboriginal people, she was elected to the safest Labor seat in the state. In her first speech to the House of Representatives on September 10, 1996, Hanson ranted that Aboriginal people enjoyed many privileges that ordinary white Australians did not have, and she claimed that Australia was in danger of being swamped by Asian immigrants.

In 1997 Hanson formed the One Nation party and published a tract, *Pauline Hanson: The Truth*, in which she presented Aboriginal people as "savage cannibals." She argued that welfare policies for Aboriginals and immigrants had divided Australians and they needed to unite again as "One Nation"—hence the name of her movement and party. Hanson called for immigration and policies of multiculturalism to be abolished, blaming immigrants for high rates of unemployment and crime. While official state policies of multiculturalism had allowed immigrants some degree of social mobility for the previous two decades, the state paid lip service to respecting cultural difference, ignoring the tensions and racial hatreds underpinning Australian society. With Hanson those tensions were coming to the fore once again. The conservative Liberal Party government led by John Howard, who had been voted into office in 1996, followed Hanson and retracted policies of multiculturalism and sought to reverse earlier land rights concessions.

As the attacks on Aboriginal people mounted during the mid- to late 1990s, black leadership was in retreat. The active and vital movement of the sixties and seventies had been driven underground or co-opted. Ten years of rule by the Labor Party had seen the formation within the state bureaucracy of a black elite known as "Abcrats," soon to be dismantled by the Howard government. The new generation of urban blackfullas, reared in the heady days of land rights marches and black power, turned to hip hop as a means of diversion and reflection as darkness descended. And, in a moment of serious crisis for an embattled community, rap came forth to speak truth to power.

"Thirty years on, it's the same old song and dance / Still no basic human rights, no chance / No economic or political voice / Like the elders of my people say, we gotta have a choice." Rapping over the top of a plaintive descending bass line and the droning sounds of a sampled didgeridoo, Waiata's voice was militant. On the cusp of the thirty-year anniversary of voting rights for Aboriginal people, little had changed. The song, "Reconciliation Crap Rap," announced the arrival and presence of a new genera- tion prepared to strike back: "We're here to assert our status, our rights / Every Black man and woman gotta stand up and fight."

The song counterposed images of strength connected with the ancestors—"barefoot and free"—and nature—"the spirit of the trees, mother earth, the beautiful creation that gave us our birth"—with the ongoing colonialist mentality of the right: "When will the ignorant Pauline Hansons understand? / There is no One Nation on blackfullas land." But Waiata also took white liberals to task for assuming that apologies could remedy the historical injustices of more than two centuries: "Not no recon- ciliation package gonna rectify the damage." And, last, she came to Aboriginal people themselves: "Blackfullas over here over on the right side / Blackfullas over there over on the left side / Blackfullas in the middle saying hey diddle diddle / Abcrats sittin' on the fence playing with their diddles." At a time when black leftists like Noel Pearson were espousing neoconservative arguments about self-reliance, and Aboriginal people pulling themselves up by their bootstraps, the boundaries between the traditional left and right seemed to be dissolving. The establishment had nothing to offer young people.

During the chorus the melody and bass line dropped out, adding heightened urgency. "Blackfulla Blackfulla why is it so / That we die so young and into prison we go? Blackfulla Blackfulla why can't you see / That the future of our children is up to you and me." The song was about the specific situation of Aboriginal people in Australia and the political juncture that they found themselves faced with. But through the music Waiata placed blackfullas in a local tradition of black resistance and a global history of oppression. The riff, "Blackfulla Blackfulla," was based on the chorus from a song by No Fixed Address, a 1970s Aboriginal reggae-rock band, with an echo of Bob Marley at the end: "We gotta stand up for our sovereign rights."

On January 26 the nation celebrates "Australia Day." The date—when Britain's First Fleet landed in Sydney Harbor in 1788—is lauded as the birth of the settler colony. Glittering bonanzas of red, white, and blue fireworks light up the sky above downtown's Darling Harbour. Crowds of thousands are entertained with live bands and testimonies from "new Australians" to mark the event. For most Aboriginal Australians the date marks the colonial encounter and centuries of brutal dispossession. To them Australia Day was better known as Invasion Day or Survival Day.

Waiata was invited to an event in Hyde Park to commemorate Australia Day in 1997. The organizers retained the colonizers' name for the holiday but were interested in making the day a gesture toward reconciliation with Aboriginal peoples. In the humid air of late January, Waiata fanned herself with a folded program as she sat through endless speeches from whites and blacks about brotherhood and tolerance. Finally, unable to contain her rising frustration, she broke with decorum and stood up, asking to speak. The host reluctantly handed over the microphone. Waiata performed her "Reconciliation Crap Rap": "Time to wipe the bullshit from our eyes / Every time we die, we're living their lies." She delivered the lines with controlled anger, to an audience of scandalized liberals and quietly indignant blackfullas.

A sense of discontent was growing among young black emcees. "Two hundred years of this bullshit / Us Kooris have had enough," rapped Brothablack. "Time for us to raise up out of the dark / From Broome all the way back to Redfern / Brothas and sistas, stand up, it's your turn."

For Ebony Williams the time had also come to speak out. On her song, "Open Up Your Mind," she painted a devastating portrait of Aboriginal Australia. "Diseases running rife in the outback communities / Because the chances of having the opportunities / Of getting food and fresh water to the people out there / It seems to me that no one cares." Over a sparse backing track consisting only of a bass and a sampled drum kit, Ebony unleashed a torrent of sharp retorts against Pauline Hanson as a "high profile trouble maker," with "no answers, no solutions," whose "mind is still filled with illusions." She alludes to Hanson's ignorance: "You say, 'I'm not a racist,' have you learnt the meaning yet?" During a 60 Minutes interview Hanson was asked if she was xenophobic, to which she replied, "Please explain?"

In media-orchestrated debates Hanson supporters were pitted against advocates of reconciliation with Aboriginal people. But to Ebony these debates legitimized the hate speech of Hanson by giving her a platform while ignoring the real issues:

> Everyone wants to have their say in the debate
> But there ain't no debate, just hate
> Our fate is in the hands of the government powers
> When all we want is what's ours.

Where are the special benefits Hanson talks about, asks Ebony, adding, "I haven't seen nothin' yet." Danielle Tuwai sang a chorus over a funky bass line: "Open up your mind, pay attention, open up your mind." The Hanson phenomenon fed on undercurrents of close-minded racism in white Australian society. Meanwhile, a new and multiracial generation was beginning to speak up and find its collective voice.

Dressed in dark blue baggy jeans, a burgundy silk shirt, and Jordans, his baby face framed by slicked-back hair, Alec Heli waited at the northeast corner of Redfern Park. He sniffed casually at his shirt, reassuring himself that he smelled decent despite his nights in the Salvation Army men's home around the corner and the quick baths he took from a trickle of cold water that spouted from a tap for a few hours every evening. Alec was being picked up on the corner by a friend from back home who was taking him to a club downtown, and Alec didn't want his friend to know that he was living in a home for vagrants. It was by chance that Waiata and I were out at the same club that night, where we met Alec for the first time.

Born in Auckland, New Zealand, of parents who had emigrated from the small Polynesian island of Niue, Alec heard stories from his cousins about the money you could make working as a bartender or a bouncer in Sydney. He had saved up the money for a ticket. But when he landed in Sydney, his cousin, who was supposed to meet him, had moved to Melbourne, and Alec didn't have money to get there. Alec was wandering along Oxford Street, hungry and alone, when he saw a homeless man climbing out from a dumpster. The fellow, who had strings of banana peel and potato chips in his hair and clothes, was slightly deranged. But he showed Alec how to scavenge for food in the narrow alleyways behind the ritzy restaurants and how to hide in the dumpsters during police raids. After a few days they were both picked up by a Salvation Army van and escorted to the men's home, where Alec slept fitfully amid the cacophony of snores, farts, and retching coughs that went on throughout the night.

Alec eventually found a room in an apartment in Leichardt and spent his days listening to music and writing rhymes. When he was growing up in New Zealand, he had joined in the b-boy frenzy in the mideighties and listened to Public Enemy and Wu-Tang Clan. By the midnineties the local New Zealand hip hop scene was thriving, from 3 The Hard Way's party anthem "Hip Hop Holiday" to the more hard-core Maori nationalist Upper Hutt Posse. Conscious of his Polynesian roots, Alec gravitated toward the Maori-Niuean rapper Che Fu and the Samoan emcee King Kapisi, who talked about European colonization of the Pacific. "The raps were my history textbooks," Alec told us. In his own rhymes he paid homage to the Maori warriors who had killed and eaten the French colonizer Marc-Joseph Marion du Fresne.

Raised on roots reggae and brought up in a Mormon household, Alec peppered his lyrics with biblical imagery of the devil, good versus evil, and divine retribution for past wrongs. With his deeply melodic voice and New Zealand lilt, he joined our group, adding soul and humor to our militant outfit. We recast ourselves as Deadly and did our first gig in February 1997 before an audience of about seven skeptical college students at Macquarie University's Multicultural Night.

But things were changing. Social forces were regrouping, young people were mobilizing, and the antiracism movement galvanized multiracial protesters across the country. The movement began to peak in 1997 when Pauline Hanson traveled around Australia, holding public meetings to set up local branches of her One Nation party. The anti-Hanson rallies brought together a large cross section of people. According to the 1996 census, 34.5 percent of the Sydney population were first-generation immigrants, as were 22.7 percent of the broader Australian population. A further 15 percent were second-generation immigrants. The changing demographics of Australian society had disrupted the White Australia fantasy; a more diverse and multiracial immigrant population was not willing to tolerate the bigotry of the past.

It was in these protests that a younger generation—beneficiaries of the voting rights legislation and more open immigration policies of the 1970s—began to come into their own. Whereas the radical movements of the sixties, such as the Vietnam War protests, were led largely by white students, the antiracism movements of the late 1990s involved many young people of color—immigrant and Aboriginal—who were involved in the day-to-day activism of organizing rallies, protest marches, and teach-ins.

In January 1997 the Rock Against Racism coalition was formed. It counted on the support of important indigenous musicians such as Tiddas, Yothu Yindi, and Kev Carmody. An annual music festival known as "Big Day Out" supported the Rock Against Racism movement, and fans and bands wore orange ribbons in solidarity.

"We're Nunga, Niuean, and Indian," announced Waiata, in front of four hundred revelers at a Sydney nightclub, the Harbourside Brasserie, at a Rock Against Racism concert. "And we're here to say no to racism."

Yet somehow it didn't feel right to me. Being Indian was a cultural and ethnic fact of who I was, not an oppositional identity like being Nunga or Niuean. Indian people were not displaced from their land for more than two hundred years or taken into slavery or economically disenfranchised as a class. Besides, I didn't really feel Indian. I hadn't grown up around any Indian people, except my family, and I was raised Catholic—I had never been to a Hindu temple or a mosque. I felt like a fraud, claiming to be Indian.

But something powerful was bringing us together, and it had more to do with the new racial geographies of a post–White Australia and the antiracist alliances that were being forged in those days. I began to think about my father's stories of how he ended up in Australia. In May 1964 he had packed all his belongings into two trunks and sailed from Bombay to London in search of work. My dad's older brother had gone to London a few years earlier, but he was away working on a boat, and he never got my dad's telegram announcing his arrival. So no one met my dad at London's Victoria Station. These were the days before the Race Relations Act made housing discrimination illegal, and as my father wandered the streets looking for a place to stay, all the "For Rent" signs carried a disclaimer: "No Asians or Blacks." He tried calling in advance, but when the landlords saw his face, they told him the rooms were taken. Eventually, an older Jewish lady rented him a room with a broken window in her attic, where he survived the bitter winter by putting newspapers between his blankets for warmth. Cold and lonely, he imagined a better life in Australia. Compared with gloomy postwar Britain, the Australia he knew through following cricket seemed a warm and welcoming place. But when he went to the Australian Consulate in London to request papers, the officials wouldn't even give him an application form. The White Australia policy was still in full effect. It wasn't until 1969 that he was permitted to apply and then received a visa. It occurred to me that these histories of border crossing and racism and rejection captured more about my life than any imaginings of my Indian ancestry.

I also began thinking about myself and my own experiences with racism in a way that I had not through the years of political activism. When I was in high school, opposition to Asian immigration was fueled by talk-radio hosts such as Ron Casey. My white classmates would say to my face that they thought Asians should go home and stop taking Aussie jobs. Some classmates told me that I acted too white, but at the same time I was expected to fit in. The strong emphasis on assimilation in Australian society had meant that identifying with your cultural background was unfashionable or uncool. My Tongan school friends dug big pits in their backyard to roast whole hogs for parties, and at home we relished the gelatinous fish eyes of my mum's signature "head curry"—things we would never talk about openly for fear of being labeled some Indiana-Jones-monkey-brains-eating freaks. At school we all ate meat pies and sang the national anthem. Talking about my experiences of white working-class racism was as embarrassing as admitting to eating fish eyes at home, and even somewhat misdirected, since I went on to college while many of my white classmates were still working low-wage jobs. But when I saw how this same racism was feeding into a white supremacist movement, it made sense to speak about it. I felt that I did have something to say, and rapping seemed to be the right way to say it.

The Sydney march was held on a crisp sunny day in late winter. More than five thousand people gathered in the downtown First Fleet Park in Circular Quay. There was a speech by an Aboriginal activist, Jenny Munro, and then a smattering of trade unionists and representatives of various ethnic organizations also spoke before we were called to the stage to perform.

I looked out onto the congregation of people, their silhouettes set against the glistening water of the bay. I saw young students in jeans and Bob Marley t-shirts, Aboriginal elders, young Muslim girls in headscarves, older Punjabi men with long kurtas and turbans, and small Vietnamese women with sun visors. Over the loudspeakers came the melodious sounds of a sitar, and then the reggae beat kicked in, with a bass descending in major thirds. "Thirty years ago in Mangalore, a young man sat looking at the shore. 'I can see my future in a foreign land, but how to leave my native sands'?" I intoned in the Indian accent of my father. The rap-reggae song related my father's experiences as he landed in a hostile London of the 1960s, then made his way to Australia, confronting ignorance and stereotypes about Asians.

Waiata and Alec joined in, singing on the chorus: "Migrants come from overseas, them that live here Aborigines," with the addition, "But we continue to fight, for land rights, to protect a sacred site, for migrant rights." The song had my father confronting the racists in an effort to unite white, brown, and black: "My skin may be brown but I'm the same as you, I've the right to live in this land too." As we sang the last chorus of the song, "You can't hide from the racist tide. You've got to stand up and fight," the crowd cheered. Three of us on stage. Three-part harmony. Nunga, Niuean, and Indian.

In retrospect the song was idealistic in imagining that we could overcome the divisions between our different communities so easily. I was buoyed by the alliances and solidarities that we were able to build during the days of the antiracism campaigns. Those alliances were crucial in helping us to counter the racist backlash. But I had also seen the racism of Asians toward Aboriginal people, the distrust between white, black, and brown. Music alone couldn't unite us across lines of race and ethnicity; we needed more on-the-ground political work and consciousness raising.

The three of us began to ask questions. Was hip hop the answer to the political vacuum we faced? Could we continue to find common ground through the music? As we worked together, we confronted more deeply the differences between Pacific Islanders, Asians, and Aboriginals. Pauline Hanson was ranting about Asians and Islanders coming to Australia and taking "Aussie jobs." In reality, Islanders and Asians were low-cost labor, who took the jobs that no one else wanted anyway. But Aboriginals were never even considered for those jobs. And as some immigrants climbed the social ladder to enjoy a middle-class existence, blackfullas were always left at the bottom. As Waiata said to us, "Islanders and Asians might be oppressed by racism, but they were not dispossessed from their land. Your family own their own land. You can hand it down from one generation to the next. You have the ability to assert your cultural identity, speak your native language. Maybe your mob come here for a Western lifestyle, money, and jobs. Nungas don't have the same luxury."

Looking back at my experiences in three cities where hip hop had put down roots, it seemed to me that the forging of a global fellowship across lines of race, ethnicity, and nation was fleeting and short-lived. It happened in spaces where black, white, and immigrant lived, worked, and partied together. It happened when the political juncture brought us together to defend a common goal. And it happened on the stage and in the music. The global fellowship allowed a Cuban rapper from Alamar to imagine his small daily struggle as part of a bigger historical movement; it gave a Nunga from Adelaide the courage and language to speak her mind when confronted with silence. But when we left behind the protest march or concert stage, the cross-racial solidarities were harder to sustain.

As the antiracism movement ebbed, flowed, and finally waned, there wasn't enough to keep the music politically engaged. Hip hop moved from the house parties and street corners of the West Side to the inner-city clubs and music festivals. It was increasingly severed from its links with race and politics by academics, music labels, and promoters, disassociated from the idea of hip hop as a "black thing." Aboriginal rappers like Wire MC, along with the Palestinian-born emcee NOMISe and female artists Maya Jupiter and Trey, worked hard to obtain recognition during this time.

As Australian hip hop went mainstream, clubs and festival organizers were less interested in message rap. A voice coach suggested that we rename our group "Alec and the Colored Girls" to appeal to a wider audience. After I left for Chicago, Alec and Waiata went to see a recording agent with a demo tape, and they were told, "No one's interested in that Public Enemy thing anymore." The only alternative, they were advised by the agent, was to become like the Aboriginal pop singer Christine Anu, a feisty diva whose upbeat dance tunes were chart toppers.

Meanwhile, was there anywhere on the planet that hip hop was still fighting the power, or was that now a thing of the past? There was still one beacon of hope. Hugo Chávez, a former paratrooper, had been elected president of Venezuela in 1998 with large-scale popular support from the urban and rural poor; he promised a revolution in the spirit of the independence leader Simón Bolívar. The Chávez government was sponsoring gatherings and festivals of hip hop artists from around the world. If hip hoppers anywhere could lead a united movement for global change, I imagined that it was there.

CHAPTER 4

In the Mouth of the Wolf

The main highway from Maiquetía International Airport to the metropolitan area of Caracas passed through the vast shantytowns in the west of the city. By night the twinkling lights of the shanties appeared like a galaxy of stars nestled in the valleys and hills. It was January 2004 and I was making the first of many trips to Caracas. My taxi continued on to the middle-class suburb of Altamira, where the driver dropped me off at the Hotel Residencia Montserrat. I spent the night in a shabby room with leaky faucets that overlooked the Parque del Este. The next morning I looked out onto happy families reclining under the shady trees with their picnic baskets and designer clothes. Where were the barrio folk, the suffering multitudes who were the supporters of the Chávez government? Certainly not here in Altamira.

The next day I called Johnny, a contact from my sister, Deepa. "Wait right there—I'm coming to get you," said Johnny. Next thing, a green Nova pulled up at the front of the hotel, Johnny in the front seat and his wheelchair in the back.

"Ocho cilindros," said Johnny, grinning as he caught me admiring the car. "This car has eight cylinders." Venezuela's major forays into auto assembly in past decades could still be seen in its citizens' pride in their cars. Johnny was a muscular, friendly Afro-Venezuelan man who had been left paraplegic after a car accident thirty years earlier. He pulled away from the curb. One hand was on the wheel, as the other reached under the seat for a bottle of Pampero Blanco rum, which he poured expertly into a plastic cup balanced between his legs while executing a left turn. He offered me the cup but I declined politely, so he drank it himself, leisurely, while driving.

Soon we had left behind the broad leafy streets of Altamira, with its secluded gardens and European-style cafes. Crossing over into the shantytowns was like entering another world—streets dense with vendors, bustling markets, improvised architecture, and the pulsing beat of reggaeton coming from transistor radios. The hills of the city were crowded with a jumble of ranchos, or precarious zinc-roofed houses with walls of carton or wood. Street kids in dirty rags sorted through piles of trash in abandoned lots.

The in-your-face poverty was at odds with the image Venezuela projected as an oil-rich nation. Even poor Caraqueños had once denied that Venezuela was a third-world country. But that was when times were better and there was enough money from petroleum to spread the wealth a bit. On February 18, 1983—otherwise known as Black Friday—a dramatic currency collapse because of falling oil prices sent the economy reeling. Desperate administrations embarked on austerity measures that shed the state of its public employees, drastically cut public spending, and deregulated prices. The result? Those living in poverty rose from 10 percent of the population in 1978 to a staggering 81 percent by 1998.[1] Those at the bottom of the social scale—mostly the black, indigenous, and mixed-race Venezuelans who form the majority of the population—were hit hardest by the changes.

The social disjunctures and crisis in governance led to spiraling violence, crime, and urban tension. In 1999 the homicide rate in Venezuela had risen 20 percent from the previous year.[2] The homicide problem was worst in Caracas, where the number of deaths sometimes reached the hundred mark on weekends. Official statistics for 2000 reported 7,779 homicides in Venezuela that year.[3]

Given the vicious cycles of poverty and violence in Venezuela, it wasn't surprising that the most popular genre among barrio youth was gangsta rap. Gangsta rap emerged in the late 1980s on the West Coast of the United States. Typically associated with artists such as NWA, Ice-T, and the Geto Boys, the genre blended storytelling and bawdy humor in its dramatization of the urban poverty and penitentiary culture of postindustrial Los Angeles. According to Eithne Quinn's booklength study of the genre, gangsta is deeply rooted in vernacular archetypes and tales taken from the black rural American South and is therefore a quintessentially African American form.[4] So how could we explain its strong appeal to barrio youth in Caracas who didn't even understand the lyrics? Did global audiences respond mainly to the rhythms of hip hop while missing the deep political and cultural symbols embedded in the music, as Imani Perry has argued?[5]

And how were gangsta rappers in Caracas responding to the movement for revolutionary change that was sweeping the country? The early 1990s saw the growth of local popular movements in the barrios. These nonpartisan movements reached a peak in 1998 when the Polo Patriótico, an alliance led by Hugo Chávez Frías, won 120 of 131 seats in the National Constituent Assembly and came into power on promises to fight corruption, break away from the US-supported neoliberal agenda, and rewrite the constitution. Encouraged by Chávez's bold speeches, the lower classes increasingly began to assert themselves. While politics until now had been dominated by white politicians from an elite class, the barrio folk finally had someone who looked like them and spoke like them, who came up like they did and understood the indignities that they suffered. And, just as Chávez was making possible new kinds of voice and representation, so too, it seemed, was the music.

My travels up until now had shown me the transient nature of the global Hip Hop Nation. Black youth in Cuba could not easily map their struggles for racial equality onto the black liberation espoused by American rappers. The underground rappers in Chicago were more concerned about protecting their hard-earned space than expanding to embrace other cultures and genders. And even the multiracial hip hoppers in Sydney could not sustain their fellowship in the absence of an antiracist political movement. I was beginning to understand that hip hop was at its best when it responded to highly local conditions. But, without broader networks, the translation of the music into politics was hard to sustain. How would that be different in a place where social movements were newly energized and supported by a leader at the very top of the system? Would rappers really have a platform here to build more enduring global linkages?

Johnny took me to the popular parish of El Valle, to the apartment he shared with his *compañera*, Yajaira. "She was in Altamira!" Johnny explained when we arrived home. "Poor thing," shrieked Yajaira, amid tumbling cascades of laughter. "Don't you worry, *chica*. We've rescued you now. Welcome to the real world."

Johnny and Yajaira lived in *bloques populares*, project-like buildings constructed by the government for barrio residents. They insisted that I sleep on a small mattress on the floor in their spare room rather than go back to my hotel room in Altamira.

The housing complex where Johnny and Yajaira lived was known as Residencia José Felix Ríbas. It was constructed for victims of a flooding tragedy in the neighboring town of La Guaira that left more than ten thousand dead and 150,000 homeless soon after Chávez came to office in 1999. Former residents of La Guaira arrived in the city to remake their lives and homes in these rapidly erected housing blocks. After several years of living in the blocks, the residents still had no cooking gas. There were frequent problems with water leakage and plumbing. There was a lack of sanitation services that produced cockroaches and rats. And in four years the complex system of gang control and drug dealing that characterizes every major barrio in contemporary Caracas had evolved.

After a few weeks of staying in the popular housing blocks, I was aware that the only reason I could move freely in the sector was because the local drug dealers had seen me with Johnny. Johnny commanded respect in their eyes because of the energetic way he lived his life despite his disability. He was a community activist who worked with street children, and he had a special rapport with the drug dealers and street children of Ríbas. The drug dealers understood that I was in the barrio as Johnny's friend, and when I arrived home in the morning or night, they left me alone. The same went for Yajaira, who had moved from barrio Marín in San Agustín to live with Johnny in El Valle a few years earlier.

Unlike the gated communities, or *urbanizaciones,* in the east of Caracas, with doormen and guards outside the front of the complexes, and then several bolted gates leading to the apartments, the housing blocks had few security gates. In Ríbas there were two main gates—one in the north of the complex and one in the east. Each building also had its own gate that led onto an open patio. The eastern gate of the complex served no real purpose. It was surrounded by low and broken-down walls, which the younger residents easily jumped to get in and out. The northern gate was monitored by the dealers, who had their drug business in a small shack at the side of the gate. The outside and inside gates were never locked because only one resident per household had the gate keys. The security for the residents of Ríbas did not lie in the locks on the gates but rather in the gangs that controlled the territory and monitored who went in and out.

The streets, patios, and doorways of the barrio were alive with children playing baseball, girls with long painted fingernails and tight shorts flirting with adolescent boys, and men playing dominoes or smoking. What underlay the relative sense of security were the arrangements between sets of competing gangs in the sector, who marked out their territory and delineated their responsibility for their area. There was even at times a sense of commitment to residents of the community. The gang leaders of Ríbas were generally on hand to assist Johnny up the ramp and through the gates, to help him push his car when it broke down, or to help Yajaira carry home her groceries.

I noticed many young men in wheelchairs—in the metro station, on the streets, and at the mall. Every time we passed one on the street, Yajaira would jokingly refer to them as "Johnny's colleagues." I asked Yajaira why there were so many young men in wheelchairs, and she told me that it was because of the violence. Yajaira had been affected by this violence personally. Her youngest brother was left paraplegic after being caught in the crossfire of an intergang dispute in San Agustín the previous year.

Some nights, the streets erupted into open warfare between competing gangs. The large holes blown by a bazooka into the facade of the local shopping mall across the road were testament to the kinds of artillery found in the barrio. Most of the time the residents joked about these intergang exchanges. When the gunshots began, the residents pretended not to notice, and, if asked, they generally used the euphemism of *fuegos artificiales*, or firecrackers, to refer to the shooting. Sadly, these kinds of shootouts could happen even during the day. They could erupt out of nowhere, and innocent residents could get caught up in the middle of a situation and be hurt or killed. It was worse when the police became involved. The Metropolitan Police, known locally as the Metropolitana, were frequently bought off by gangs. But police often made incursions into the barrio, disrupting the relative equilibrium established by the gangs. A few times when we came home late we saw the security forces with their semiautomatics held to the backs of kids, pressing them up against the walls of the barrio buildings. "Just keep walking," Johnny would say. "Don't give them eye contact."

A ella le gusta la gasolina, Da me mas gasolina, Como le encanta la gasolina, Da me mas gasolina." The infectious, grinding reggaeton of Daddy Yankee played over and over on the *minitecas*—the portable DJ stands that lined the crosswalk from Ríbas to the El Valle metro stop. The *minitecas* were interspersed among individual stalls piled high with underwear, jeans, children's toys, electronics, and candy. Vendors sold papaya, pineapples, mangoes, green beans, yuca, and tomatoes, as well as pastries, doughnuts, and household cleaning products. From portable food carts came the scent of sweet corn and butter as vendors prepared *arepas*, small corn cakes with savory fillings; *cachapas*, thick corn pancakes stuffed with cheese; and sizzling fried plantains.

The music vendors displayed several rows of pirated CDs in small plastic casings with black-and-white photocopied cover sleeves. Each CD sold for 3,000 bolívares, about US$1.40. The vendors would purchase the latest CD releases—by Celia Cruz, Marc Anthony, and Shakira—along with blank CDs and plastic covers in bulk at the cavernous underground markets in the Plaza Diego Ibarra. The same CDs sold brand new in the middle-class shopping centers such as the Centro Sambil for 15,000 bolívares, or US$7.00. But their largest distribution was through these pirated copies, which accounted for about 75 percent of the total sales of a disc when it was released.

I asked at one of the stands if they had any local hip hop CDs. The vendor showed me a disc released in 2001, *Venezuela subterránea* (Venezuela Underground), a showcase of Venezuela's underground hip hop. He then pulled out two other CDs. One album, *La realidad mas real* (The reality more real), was by a group called Guerrilla Seca. Two young black men stood back to back, and an English label reading "Parental Advisory, Explicit Lyrics" was superimposed over the tip of one rapper's middle finger, raised in an obscene gesture. On the other disc, *Papidandeando* (Partying) by Vagos y Maleantes, there was a label in Spanish that read, "Pendiente activo, grado maloso" (Active attention, bad rating). Faced with the threat of a federal mandate, the US record industry had begun slapping labels warning parents about explicit lyrics on hard-core rap and other recordings in the mid-1980s. In Venezuela such labels were added by rappers themselves to give a stamp of authenticity. On the back cover of *Papidandeando*, the rappers appeared as elaborately decked-out hustlers, in pin-striped suits, gold chains, and dark sunglasses, with designer sneakers and expensive watches.

Curious, I picked up all three CDs. How could I find out more about these rappers, their label, and underground hip hop in Venezuela? Everyone pointed me to José Roberto Duque, a novelist and chronicler of Venezuelan hip hop.

Duque pulled up outside our block in a dusty red Toyota. He was round and freckled, with kind, crinkly eyes, and when he laughed his whole body shook. While breezing through the streets of Caracas, we started talking hip hop, and I mentioned the Sugar Hill Gang's "Rapper's Delight."

"Coño!" exclaimed Duque. "You know when we heard that song back in 1979, we were blown away by the style of rhyming and the catchy beat. But it was so long and incomprehensible to us that it was rebaptised 'La cotorra,' which is a verbose, tedious speech. A year later, this one *tipo* [guy], Perucho Conde from the barrio of Caricuao, made up a version of the song called 'La cotorra criolla.'" Duque started rapping with a frenetic energy to the rhythm of Rapper's Delight: "Los cuatro reales que uno se gana, me los pagan hoy y no llegan a mañana. Mi mujercito tanto que se afana, pa' llenar la olla o la palangana" (The four bucks that you make, they pay you one day and it don't make it till tomorrow. My little woman works till late, to put food in the pan and on the plate). "That was the first rap recorded in Spanish."

Duque began with a tour of the wealthy neighborhoods in the east of Caracas. We drove through an upper-class suburb called La Lagunita. Multistory houses were barely visible through elaborate grills and security apparatuses, some with private guards stationed at the entrances. Cars with tinted windows moved silently past. We could have just as easily been in Beverly Hills. The upper classes in Venezuela were largely the descendants of Europeans. They spoke American-accented English—often because they were educated in American schools—and did their shopping in Miami. If not for their Venezuelan passports, it would be easy to mistake them for white Americans.

On my left Duque pointed out the colonial architecture, palms, and carefully manicured lawns of the Caracas Country Club. The walls surrounding the country club featured graffiti in places. I looked with surprise at the elaborate, detailed block letters that sprang up from the dusty pavement in a palette of pinks, reds, and blues.

"No *chamo* [kid] from the barrio could afford the expensive spray cans to do this kind of graffiti. And they'd be chased out of here in a minute." Duque had read my thoughts. "So it's mostly the middle-class kids that do it."

But why would the country club permit kids—even middle-class kids—to paint its outside walls with hip hop graffiti? When I looked closer at the graffiti, I noticed that some of it was political. There were images of the Venezuelan flag and slogans urging people to sign a petition for a recall referendum that would oust Chávez from power. "With your signature you decide," read the block letters. Those tags were signed "Primera Justicia," one of the main opposition parties, which must have commissioned the graffiti. Large sectors of the middle and upper classes—like those who lived in La Lagunita and played golf at the country club—were opposed to Chávez and his campaign of radical redistribution. Opposition parties had participated in the short-lived coup against Chávez in 2002 and were now hoping to get rid of him through the recall referendum.

It was a far cry from the graffiti pioneers in New York City who jacked spray cans, scaled the steel beams to elevated subway stations and train yards, and created their pieces under the cover of night. Here, kids from wealthy families were being paid to deface the walls of one of the most prestigious clubs in the city. And they were using the defiant styles and language of hip hop to defend their enclaves of privilege.

From the east of the city we made our way over to the west, to the parish 23 de Enero where Duque lived. El Veintitrés, as it was known, was a strong contrast to the ostentatious wealth of La Lagunita. The parish consisted mainly of high-rise projects, constructed by the dictator Marcos Pérez Jimenez in the 1950s for rural migrant workers coming into the city. We passed one entrance at Avenida Sucre, where there was a mural of the Argentine rebel Che Guevara next to a masked guerrilla with the message "Welcome to 23 de Enero." Duque pointed out the bullet marks in the facades of several buildings, a reminder of the tragic days following the 1989 Caracazo riots when barrio folk rose up against increasing costs of transportation fares and the army was deployed to the streets of the capital to quell the disturbances.

We took another entrance to the parish by the metro stop Agua Salud, which let out at a busy avenue. Street vendors sold newspapers and fresh fruits, hawked trinkets, and offered telephone services. Buses and cars choked the busy street and collected waiting lines of passengers, headed for the sector called Monte Piedad.

As Duque drove up the road to Monte Piedad, a housing project of fifteen-story buildings set against hills and bulbous clouds came into view. Laundry hung from the windows, fluttering in the breeze. The road wound up toward the top of the hill as we approached Monte Piedad Arriba. Here, a cultural organization, the Coordinadora Cultural Simón Bolívar, had its headquarters in an abandoned building. Facing the building was a wall that bore a series of fierce images of indigenous chiefs. There were also murals of young men from the barrio who were killed in combat with the national guard. The murals of fallen comrades, and bullet holes in the facades of the buildings, gave the sense of being in a war zone.

Duque explained that El Veintitrés had been a focal point for the guerrilla movement that emerged during the 1960s, when the dictatorship ended and a highly constrained democracy was put in place. Inspired by the Cuban revolution, leftists and revolutionaries in the barrios began to form guerrilla units. Duque grew up in the midst of this developing urban insurgency. As a kid, he would see the urban-guerrilla snipers on the rooftops of the project buildings and would join in by throwing stones at the cops.

By the time Duque was a teenager, the combat between urban guerrillas and the security forces had been replaced by conflict between gang members and the police. As crack circulated in the poorer neighborhoods in large quantities during the 1980s, several former guerrillas left behind militant politics and entered the drug trade. Leftist activists with experience in expropriating territory, using arms, and planning military operations began to use these techniques to their own benefit, setting up small drug cartels in the barrios and staking claim to their territories.

A new generation of urban youth was drawn into the drug trade at a time when other options, such as manual labor and education, were increasingly unavailable. Young barrio males were attracted by the rebellious and cool image of the *malandro* —an archetypal figure who was an outlaw or gangster. Venezuelan rappers like Guerrilla Seca reworked the folk symbol of the *malandro* just as American gangsta rappers drew on the vernacular figure of the "badman," as a representation of anti-assimilation, black insurgency, and stylized violence.[6] But the lifestyle of the *malandro* was also a death sentence, condemning young men to violent futures on the streets.[7] During the 1990s the state formed paramilitary units trained for urban combat. In 1994 they created urban squads known as the Angeles Guardianes (Guardian Angels), based on civil security forces that formed at the end of the 1970s in the US. The phrase "Plomo Contra el Hampa," or War Against Delinquency, became part of every politician's repertoire and a justification for violent death and incarceration at the hands of the state. There were numerous parallels between histories of law enforcement in North and South America and the cultural tropes that developed in response. There was a reason why barrio youth in Caracas were drawn to American gangsta rap, and it was not just the rhythms. The bleakness and despondency of the music echoed the deteriorated social fabric of their lives.

As the white middle and upper classes in La Lagunita and Altamira barricaded themselves within their gated fortresses, calling for more severe penalties against delinquency, rappers taunted them with songs like Guerrilla Seca's "Llegó el hampa" (The delinquents have arrived). The track begins with an upbeat all-female chorus announcing, "Murderers, murderers, the murderers have arrived," followed by a fast-paced rap: "Die! Don't mess with us because we are guerrillas." The rappers play on white fears of violent blacks' descending from the dreaded *cerros*, or hillside shanties: "It makes you nervous when you see this black coming down from the *cerros* shooting," and "You know that I am your nightmare." The song ends with the chorus "Nobody escapes from Guerrilla Seca. Careful, the delinquents have arrived!"

Gangsta rappers in Venezuela clearly had some things to say. But unlike the middle-class kids who were doing graffiti, poor kids from the barrio didn't have resources. Where did they get the money to buy the samplers to make beats? How did they have the connections to distribute their CDs?

Subterránea Records—Underground Records in English— was not how you would imagine the home of an underground record label in a poor country. Juan Carlos Echeandía, the founder of the label, was not how you would imagine the founder of Venezuela's most popular underground hip hop label. The offices of Subterránea Records were in a tower complex in Altamira. Duque and I entered the cool, air-conditioned offices and found art deco chairs and tables, panoramic views of the city, and a professional staff. Echeandía, a young, clean-cut, white Venezuelan in an Ecko shirt, came over to introduce himself. While we talked, his attention was constantly being diverted by phone calls and requests from the staff.

"I am a publicist," Juan Carlos explained to us. "This is my profession. But I was bored with being a publicist, producing commercials for television, always doing the same thing. I knew this guy called Bostas Brain, one of the members of the first hip hop group in Venezuela, La Corte. I told him that I had the urge to do something personal, artistic. It could be a documentary. Bostas told me, 'Do it on hip hop.' He told me about a place here in Caracas where all the rappers, gangstas, *graffiteros*, and DJs meet. It's called the Paseo los Próceres—a park that's a monument to all the heroes of independence. So I went. I liked it. In truth, I liked it because I was attracted to the 'look' of the rappers, their baggy pants, their bandannas."

Juan Carlos continued, "So I started out by investigating the culture, and then I made a documentary, *Venezuela subterránea: cuatro elementos, una música* (Underground Venezuela: Four elements, one music). That was where I joined with DJ Trece, the protagonist of the documentary. After that I was inclined to work with Trece, and we produced the disc *Venezuela subterránea*. We produced the disc in a bathroom that we converted into a studio—that was where we recorded the voices. The bedroom was our base of operations for the sound engineer. Something completely *under*.

"The disc went to the streets and it was a huge success. It had a national impact; people started listening to it in many cities of the interior. Here there is a strong market in piracy, which is clearly really hard for those of us who have the initiative to enter into this market. But at the same time it's given us a lot of opportunities. Piracy multiplies your work; it makes the groups known. When we go to cities like Maracaibo, Valencia, Barquisimeto, people know our songs and you'd never guess that they would. After the success of *Venezuela subterránea*, I left my work as a publicist and I dedicated myself to producing CDs and managing rap groups. I started up Subterránea Records, and we produced two more discs, *La realidad mas real*, by Guerrilla Seca and *Papidandeando*, by Vagos y Maleantes, the two groups that were featured on *Venezuela subterránea*."

He went on: "It also so happened that the entry of the movement of hip hop here in Venezuela coincided with a range of political changes. In some ways the popular masses begin to have voice and vote. Within these changes the poor majority begin to have much more importance in political and social life. And this is also what happens vis-à-vis the discs. That is, the marginalized now have opportunities to express themselves via the music. The rappers identify their own narratives of poverty, violence, and social difference with the political discourse of President Chávez."

Juan Carlos confirmed what I had expected to find in Venezuela: that gangsta rap here—much like the "classic gangsta" of the West Coast in the States—had a political message, and gangsta rappers were part of the movement spurred on by Chávez.[8] So what if that message was being brought by white publicists in Altamira? Wasn't that how things had always worked for black artists?

"In the US there is a distinction between commercial and underground rap," Juan Carlos added. "Rap has become a decadent movement. It was born from a very noble spirit and now prostitutes itself as a money-making machine, independent of talent. But in Venezuela we can't talk in the same terms. If the mass media and sales of discs determine whether any group is considered underground or commercial, then my groups have become commercial. But I think that a group such as Guerrilla Seca is more underground than any other in the sense of content. If you talk about realities that are not known by the mass public via music, I think that this is respecting the message of hip hop, although commercial distribution is helping to bring that message." And with that he was whisked away by his secretary, a young woman with manicured nails who wore a tailored suit.

Venezuelan rappers from the barrio were reliant on middle-class publicists and producers to produce their music and to help them access the market. Drug money was too erratic to finance the expenses of album production. There were few community-outreach arts programs. And because Caracas was not on the tourist circuit, there were no foreigners to bring samplers and other equipment. But perhaps another reason why gangsta rappers turned to these middle-class professionals was because they wanted to make money. The rappers saw the commercial potential of exploiting their ghetto realities for profit, and they ran with it.

In person Pedro Pérez, aka Budu, of Vagos y Maleantes was a sweet, brown-skinned, round-faced young man. Nothing like his album cover image of a traditional gangster packing a 9mm handgun. Carlos Madera was a tall, lean guy with a thin moustache. Madera's stage name, El Nigga, was borrowed from American gangsta rap vernacular, where the term has been pervasive and often controversial. Robin Kelley says that gangsta rappers' spelling of the word as *nigga*, rather than the the derogatory *nigger*, points to a new collective identity shaped by class, police repression, and poverty.[9] That might suggest why it resonated with barrio youth. Budu and El Nigga had grown up in Calle Carabobo of the barrio San José de Cotiza, known ominously as *la boca del lobo*, or the mouth of the wolf. They listened to Ice-T, Afrika Bambaataa, Run-

© Sara Maneiro

Budu and Nigga of Vagos y Maleantes. Cotiza, Caracas, 2003

© Sara Maneiro

Budu and Nigga of Vagos y Maleantes. Cotiza, Caracas, 2003

DMC, and Snoop Dogg, and while they enjoyed the music and the rhythms, they didn't understand any of the words. The lyrical content of rap music traveled to them via Puerto Rico, and rappers such as Vico C, who rapped in Spanish. Vagos y Maleantes was also heavily influenced by *salsa brava*, a bass-heavy, jazz-inspired form of salsa, popularized by groups in the

1970s and 1980s, such as Hector Lavoe, Eddie Palmieri, and the Fania All Stars.

Budu first became involved in hip hop through b-boy culture, which arrived in Venezuela in the early '80s. He belonged to a crew and would spend all his time at b-boy battles in the towers of Parque Central and in Sabana Grande. The next phase to come along was hip hop videos and rap. "The first group that I bought in vinyl was Run-DMC," said Budu. "They were the first ones to impact me with their song 'Walk This Way,' with Aerosmith." As Budu was talking, I thought back to my own first music cassette in Australia—*Hits of Summer 87*—and how the same Run-DMC song had grabbed my attention as a teenager.

"The moment arrived where I thought that hip hop culture would be implanted here in Venezuela. Then it disappeared in the nineties, I don't know what happened," explained Budu. "But hip hop culture always remained with me," he continued. "I would buy the discs, dance in my house, and I always had the faith that this movement would return. I continued in the streets, in my own thing, but I always listened to hip hop music, as well as salsa, jazz, and funk. El Nigga was a poet. His father was in the mafia, and I remember there'd be gatherings of those mafia types. They called El Nigga to do his poetry for his father's friends, all of them drunk. One day we saw these *panas* [friends] from the group El Corte, and we liked the way the audience moved, the presence of the rapper, the music, and we realized that we liked it. He and I began to write. We began to make music and we began to record.

"One day we got a call from DJ Trece. He invited us to his studio to record a song. We went, and I think we were the first group here in Venezuela to do gangsta rap—talking about the doctrine of the streets, something that had a strong impact in the Caracas underground and in all of Venezuela. The song had an impact. We thought we'd be able to record a disc, but, no, it was all for nothing. The disc didn't come out. Trece fought with his manager. The group dissolved, and the disc was not produced. So we went back to the bottom, to the streets again.

"We were thinking, there's no one who'll support us, nobody can pay for a studio for us. Well, let's sell drugs to pay for our own production. So we took turns standing on the street corner below. They'd say, 'Hey, deliver this for me,' and so on. And in this way we recorded six songs, paying for them ourselves, until the day that Juan Carlos Echeandía came with his proposal of a documentary, *Venezuela subterránea*. He must have been sent by God. We were practically ready to go into jail, because the police would see me, recognize me, and they'd say, 'We're going to take you, we're tired of this.' They had shut down my bodega. I had a business and they shut me down."

Vagos y Maleantes, as Budu and Nigga called themselves, was a play on a 1956 law known as Ley sobre vagos y maleantes (Law for vagrants and criminals). The law was devised during the military regime of Pérez Jiménez in order to imprison dissidents and later those considered undesirables by the authorities. But in reality Budu and Nigga didn't want the life of vagrants and criminals. They wanted the stability of work and family that was always out of reach. "In the barrios there's a lot of violence, every day more violence," said Budu. "But what we want is to end delinquency. What we want is more sources of work. What we want is for our children to have an education."

After hearing DJ Trece mentioned several times, I was curious to meet him. I barraged Duque with questions. What was Trece's background? How did he get started? Where did he get the equipment to produce beats? Duque just shrugged his shoulders in response.

Juan Carlos arranged for Duque and me to appear on DJ Trece's weekly hip hop radio show. We took the elevator up to the tenth floor of the Ateneo de Caracas, an arts center close to downtown. The doors opened onto a small lobby where some rappers were sitting on a couch. Outside speakers carried the perky voice of the R&B singer Kelis: "My milkshake brings all the boys to the yard / And their life, it's better than yours. Damn right, it's better than yours."

We could see DJ Trece speaking into a microphone in a

studio inside. He was a tall white guy with longish brown hair. He lined up another song, and then his assistant ushered us in. Trece rose, shook hands with us, and spoke in English, "Hey, yo, what's up?" Duque rolled his eyes at me; he didn't understand any English.

As we settled into the seats, Trece continued addressing us in English. It seemed that Trece was trying to upstage Duque in front of the foreigner, show him to be just another guy from the barrio, while Trece flaunted his international credentials. I tried to steer the conversation back to Spanish, so that Duque wouldn't feel left out. But Trece was determined to speak in English.

Trece proudly told me that he was born in New York, while his mother was doing a PhD at New York University, and he grew up in Greenwich Village. He studied visual arts at the Nova Scotia College of Art and Design, later transferring to the San Francisco Art Institute. After graduating from college, he became involved in hip hop culture and moved to Mexico to become a DJ. In Mexico he learned how to make beats, then returned to Venezuela to become a producer. He began working with Guerrilla Seca and Vagos y Maleantes. "These guys coming from the streets were *malandros*," he said. "They wanted to be an artist like me, but they grew up in a different environment that wasn't so artistic."

"In ninety-seven, when I came back to Venezuela," Trece continued, "people didn't even know the word *DJ* or *hip hop*. I was the only DJ in this era. So through the radio I decided to make my own network. The movement of hip hop began to grow and evolve and awaken the barrios. I was a catalyst. I acted as a jump-start for the movement to begin. That is, I'm the one responsible for hip hop in Venezuela. *Y al mismo tiempo*," he said, slipping back into Spanglish, "I found in hip hop the right brush for my art. It wasn't oil painting or sculpture making or photography. It was hip hop."

I could now see the reason for Duque's earlier evasiveness about Trece. It was not just that Trece was egotistical, but his account of hip hop's development in Venezuela seemed typical of many origin narratives of global hip hop, in that it excluded the people who had been part of the first waves of hip hop culture, who had participated as b-boys and rappers from the very beginning. It was another way of making people like Duque and Budu invisible, and of giving all credit to the people who brokered hip hop's entrance into the mainstream. But, while hip hop was a personal project for Juan Carlos, or an artistic medium for Trece, for the rappers in the barrios the music was much more than that—it was what they lived.

"If hip hop started as a black and Latino movement," continued Trece—at least he acknowledged that much (for all of his professed education, Trece seemed remarkably ignorant of the African American history and culture that gave rise to his "paintbrush")—"now it's amazing that there are no limitations, and that is my first line, no limitations. And there are people who can prove that. You see it with Eminem and DJ Shadow, for example, one of the biggest beat-making scientists there is. And he is a white kid from the suburbs. And Elvis Presley, for instance, how he translated black music. Eminem is like an Elvis Presley. No limitations and anything is possible, anything goes. If you want to rap about bling bling, that's cool. If you want to rap about politics, that's cool. If you want to rap about sex, that's cool. It doesn't bother me."

The song Trece was playing was coming to an end, and he reached for another CD—Vagos y Maleantes' *Papidandeando*. He positioned the CD to a track he had produced, "Historia nuestra" (Our history), and he hit *play*. Suddenly, the room vibrated with the brassy tones of a buoyant salsa beat. Then Budu's voice rapping:

> From a kid, I was raised in the barrio, or in other words, hell
> Where nobody is immortal
> Get comfortable and listen to the biography of these two guys
>   ...
> My mama works hard without rest
> My father abandoned me when I was a kid
> I don't care 'cause I don't need him
> At seventeen, I got sick for money, and I started to deal drugs

A different environment, other life
Now people see me like a real delinquent ...
The problems were abundant in my nuclear family
They dreamed of me being an engineer, and I dreamed of
  being a criminal

There was something jarring about Trece's upbeat salsa music and Budu's dark lyrics. They didn't seem to fit together. I thought back to all the other producers I knew—Pablo, Munkimuk, Khaled, DJ Presyce—all people who came from the same marginal communities as the rappers they produced, and whose beats allowed the lyrics to speak in all their pain and poetry. But in Venezuelan hip hop, where commerce and privilege met the harsh realities of the streets, the dissonance of the music was itself an expression of the unbridgeable divide that existed out there in the city.

The central district of Caracas was covered in a haze of black smoke. On the Avenida Baralt a vehicle of the Metropolitana was going up in bright orange flames, its molten core giving way to gray and black plumes of smoke that filled the atmosphere and choked our lungs. All the way down the street and in side alleys, people burned motorcycles belonging to the Metropolitana. They set fire to advertisements for Polar beer—a company owned by the billionaire Gustavo Cisneros, who had helped to finance the 2002 coup against Chávez. Bystanders watched, some chanted slogans, and the police looked on from the distant fringes, afraid or unwilling to intervene.

The palpable anger arose from an announcement that day, June 3, by the National Electoral Council (CNE) that the opposition had gathered the 2.4 million signatures needed to trigger a referendum on whether to recall Chávez from power. The referendum was scheduled for August 15. But just a few months earlier the CNE had ruled that one-third of the signatures presented by the opposition were not valid. The CNE had made the lists public and gave the opposition five days in May to validate the signatures. Barrio folks who supported Chávez were appalled to find that the opposition had fraudulently used their names or had used the names of their long-dead parent or uncle. Yet despite efforts of people to purge these names, the CNE ruled that the opposition had gathered sufficient signatures and the referendum would go ahead. It was a slap in the face for an underclass that had been swindled by powerful groups one time too many. As I stood watching the streets go up in flames, I received a text message from Johnny: "*Camarada, nos jodieron*" (Comrade, they screwed us).

During June and July barrio folks accepted the hard reality that the recall referendum would go ahead. They set about organizing a "Vote NO" campaign in the streets and in the barrios that would ensure a massive turnout of Chávez supporters to vote against recall. The shantytowns were the site of fervent preparations as residents set up voter registration centers, organized colorful marches and parades, and went door to door to enlist support. The cultural establishment—now nominally Chavista—also joined in the efforts. On August 6 the cultural establishment organized a rap concert in the Poliedro stadium, billed as the First International Festival of Youth Music. The slogan was "Say NO to Drugs"—a thinly veiled attempt to incorporate the Chavista referendum slogan.

I arrived at the Poliedro with Duque, Yajaira, and Mike Walsh from Chicago—who was now my husband and was visiting me in Caracas. The three-thousand-capacity stadium was almost filled. The audience was mostly young people from the barrios—brown and black skinned, clad in hip hop gear. Outside there were vendors selling cans of beer. The alcohol fueled a heady mixture of masculine aggression and youthful energy as the young men jostled one another in the vast open floor space in front of the stage that was known as the *parte baja*. We took our seats in the rear mezzanine, overlooking the scene.

An hour passed with no signs of any bands coming onto the stage. Young people in the *parte baja* were starting to get drunk. Periodically, they would propel half-empty beer cans across the room. From the upper levels it was a spectacle to see hundreds of beer cans rocketing around the *parte baja*, the yeasty odor of spilled beer combining with the sweaty stench of crowded bodies.

Finally, the first group for the night began setting up. They were a rock group from Colombia. As these white boys with guitars and long hair began a mellow ballad, the audience was restless. The *rockeros* began a second song, a more upbeat rock song. The young people in the audience started to become agitated. Halfway through the song they shouted at the performers, "*Fuera, fuera*" (Get off, get off), and threw beer cans and other debris at the musicians. The guitarists stopped playing and castigated the audience: "You are a bunch of uneducated kids. You have no respect."

Yajaira, Duque, and I looked incredulously at each other. How could the organizers have enlisted a white rock band to play before this crowd of barrio youth? While rock music was popular among middle-class kids, in the macho culture of barrio youth it was derided as *guachu-guachu*, rejected as sissy or effeminate. As Duque put it in his liner notes for the *Venezuela subterránea* disc, "In the '70s, a *malandro* who listened to the Bee Gees was like a 45-caliber handgun covered in Hello Kitty stickers." In the barrios it was the *tambores*, the infectious rhythms of salsa, and now rap and reggaeton, that were popular.

Things went from bad to worse. More white rock groups from Colombia and Argentina were booed off the stage. Each group took a long time to set up. There were sound and technical problems. Tension and frustration mounted in the *parte baja*, as the youth consumed more beer, and fights began to break out.

Then one of the organizers—Noel Marquez from the Afro-Venezuelan drumming group Grupo Madera—came onto the stage. Grupo Madera members were strong supporters, even spokespersons, for the Chávez government; their hit song "Uh ah Chávez no se va" (Uh ah Chávez won't go) was the anthem of the Chavista movement.

"Who is Chavista here?" shouted Marquez. There was a feeble response. "Who is Bolivariano here?" A scattering of people raised their hands. Marquez left the stage, satisfied that he had placated the crowd while the sound engineers worked to fix some technical problems. But as time went on, the young people grew more impatient. Marquez kept reappearing on the stage, yelling, "Who is Bolivariano?" "Who will vote NO?" People started to get annoyed with Marquez at this point, and they pelted him with beer cans. "OK," he said, holding his hands in the air in surrender. "We're going to give you some rap." The audience paused, its expectations raised momentarily.

The first rap act was Actitud Maria Marta, a white rapper from Argentina known for her political raps. There was a buzz of amusement in the crowd as she climbed on to the stage. Her translucent white skin was artificially tanned, and her straight brown hair was braided into cornrows. The organizers couldn't give the crowd any black performers—that was insult enough— but to now give them a white rapper in blackface? Maria Marta began her first song in a shouting rap, revealing her origins in the punk rock of the 1980s. But she paused halfway through, aware that she had lost the audience. Lacking the arrogance of the earlier male groups, she quietly left the stage.

Next on were DJ Trece and a blond punk rapper named Belica. Belica's eyes were bloodshot and she had trouble standing up straight. "*Anda fumao*," Yajaira observed wryly—Belica was high. Trece rapped in Spanglish: "With *sabor Latino agresivo*, you know my *estilo* / Like *estilo neoyorquino*, baby, baby, listen to this / Come on, once again, I do it like this / Move your body, I'm ready for the party." Belica swayed unsteadily on the stage to the music, unable to coordinate her movements to pick up the microphone. It was a farce—the drugged-out performer, the marijuana being smoked around us, and all this at a "Say NO to Drugs" concert. Trece continued with his lame rap, until finally the audience had enough. "*Fuera, fuera*," they shouted. Duque and I exchanged smiles. It was somewhat gratifying to see the self-proclaimed founder of Venezuelan hip hop tuck his tail between his legs and walk off the stage in defeat.

The situation in the *parte baja* was growing more volatile. The shoving and jostling were getting vicious. Suddenly, a gunshot rang out. There was silence in the auditorium. Then people started running toward the exits and screaming. A space gradually cleared around a fallen body to the left of the stage. People watched in quiet dismay as a stretcher arrived and paramedics removed the lifeless form. Then the audience slowly reassembled on the floor, much more subdued than before.

"Welcome to the mouth of the wolf / Where in less than a second anything can happen / Murders, attacks, that is daily life in my barrio / Day and night, night and day," El Nigga rapped in a low growl as he came up on the stage. The rap was accompanied by a discordant and ominous-sounding riff. The audience immediately became attentive. People clamored around the front of the stage, hanging on to every word. "Calle Carabobo, a labyrinth without exit / A subterranean zone where the mafia reigns / You can't avoid the bullets, they rise and fall / That's what it's like where I live."

After Vagos y Maleantes, the rappers Colombia and Requesón from Guerrilla Seca were up with their song "Black Malandreo." Colombia sported a green-and-gold Celtics cap and shirt, and Requesón had on a Los Angeles Clippers hat. "I go on desperately, looking for work is a joke," rapped Requesón. "I make it home, my kids are crying. What's happening, my situation is getting worse."

"Brother, what's happening?" asked Colombia.

"The hunger is killing us," responded Requesón.

"Well, what are you thinking?

"I have my house, my kids crying of hunger and the pain that envelops me / What I want is to buy half a kilo of drugs and start a business."

"The same thing will happen to you that happened to me."

"To me! Don't you see that I don't give a shit anymore, and I'm talking to you in confidence / It's not for me but for my kids who have nothin.'"

"Guerrilla Seca represents, misery, poverty, shit," they rapped together on the chorus. "This is the reality that can happen to you / What I live is *malandreo*, this is the real story."

A hush had extended over the audience. I watched the faces of

the young people in the crowd, drawn into the story that Guerrilla Seca was telling. It was their story. It struck me that this
was one thing that the government didn't understand. Young
people were hungering for representation and recognition, and
that didn't always come with political slogans. Sometimes it
just came when someone gave voice to their experiences. And
despite Chávez's tremendous appeal to the masses, the cultural
establishment was Eurocentric and out of touch with young
people. Like these politicians, I had jumped the proverbial gun
in expecting that gangsta rappers in Caracas would naturally be
a part of a movement for revolutionary change. But, as Robin
Kelley and others have warned in the context of the US, before
deciding how gangsta rappers might or might not act politically,
we first had to understand where they were at.

Colombia and Requesón were much more subdued than
Budu and Nigga. When we met in the offices of Subterránea
Records, they spoke in low and somber tones, just like their
hard-core and gritty music. Their influences were the American
rappers Tupac, Nas, and Ludacris. Like the rappers from Vagos y
Maleantes, they couldn't understand the English lyrics, but they
said that there was a certain flow, a feeling associated with the
music, that spoke to them.

When Requesón was twelve years old, he was part of the rap
group Aracnorap, whose members would meet at Parque del
Oeste and rhyme in the street. Several members of the group
were lost to drug addiction or imprisoned, and Requesón continued on his own. He later formed another duo with a rapper from
the group La Realeza, but that rapper was wrongly convicted
of murder and imprisoned shortly thereafter. It was then that
Requesón met Colombia—the son of Colombian immigrants
—at a club in el 23 de Enero, and they began to perform
together. After winning a rhyming competition at a club in the
middle-class neighborhood of Las Mercedes in 1999, Requesón
and Colombia formed the group Guerrilla Seca. They would
freestyle together in Los Próceres, where they were eventually
introduced to Juan Carlos.

Colombia and Requesón of Guerrilla Seca. Los Próceres, Caracas, 2003

I was glad to have the chance to sit down with Colombia and Requesón. There was a question that had been bothering me, and it was something that I wanted to ask them. I had listened to their CD *La realidad mas real* countless times, and the themes of poverty, oppression, police brutality, and racism seemed to overlap with the concerns of underground rappers I had encountered around the world. It was satirical, caustic social commentary. But one song on the album seemed wildly out of place, "Voy a hacer plata" (I'm going to make money). The lyrics of this song sounded like something on the airwaves of New York's Hot 97 FM: "I'm going to make money / From when you're born till when you die, that's what it's about," and "If I could make five million dollars a month I'd be a real millionaire / ... I'd get gold teeth and I'd adorn myself in gold all over. I'd have a ton of Rolex, rings, chains for daily use." And the last line truly offended my sensibilities as a feminist: "I'm going to make money, *whore*."

"I just don't get it," I told the rap duo. "The music all made sense till I got to that track. Why the focus on materialism and money as the ultimate goal?"

"The song talks about what we—today's generation—what we want and what we crave," Colombia began. "We're clear that we live in a very materialist world and that the world of money is the focus. If the world was not so upside down, if everything was not about money, if everything was not so materialistic—"

Requesón chimed in: "We're clear that we ourselves are not materialists, but we've never had anything. We are poor and we believe that we deserve something also for all our work. We are people who live in a barrio. We live in bad conditions and we want to get ahead, take our mothers out of poverty. We talk of money and Rolex watches and gold teeth because we don't have these things. We know there are things more important to sing about than a watch or a car. There are more important things like war or hunger. But we have to orient ourselves to where the conversation is at, because we want people to listen to us, and we want to bring reality into focus."

Gangsta rappers were aware that they were coming of age in an era when personal worth was increasingly measured in terms of consumption and status symbols. If their potent brand of gangsta rap gave voice to experiences of marginality and poverty in an era of aggressive free-market capitalism, they also saw the free market as the only way to rise out of poverty. And the enterprise of making money was bound up with their masculinity and assertion of male dominance, as seen in their troubling references to women as whores. But as they spoke, I noticed the subtext of a more complex story about the degradations of class and race. The market was not just a way out of poverty but a way to prove one's worth and dignity as a human being in a society in which young black men from the barrio are treated as less than human.

"Now we are professionals and we can move up in life," Requesón continued. "We want people to see us and respect us, or at least see that we are trying to move forward. You have something; you have earned something with your work and through your struggle."

"The truth is that we, blacks, have always been oppressed," Colombia said. "Racism exists in all countries. Here they'll 'blacken' you just because of the clothes you wear. You get on a bus, and they look at you like, Is he going to rob me? But we have to fight to show that not all blacks are *malandros,* and not all blacks are delinquents, and not all blacks are involved in drug trafficking."

Requesón agreed. "One hundred thousand people see you like that. Blacks *are* those who live in the barrio. Blacks *are* those who have suffered. Blacks *are* those who live in this world of violence. But they treat us like we're the bad ones because we're poor, because we don't have anything. And I think we deserve respect."

Colombia and Requesón's assertion of black identity seemed to go against long-held myths that Venezuela was a *café con leche,* or coffee with milk, society, where all races coexisted and blended harmoniously. Even though there was tremendous segregation among the races, Venezuelans didn't have a tendency to see themselves in racial terms. Was race just an idea that hip hop culture was introducing? Or, as in Cuba, did hip hop give voice to divisions that were growing more acute with economic crisis? For Requesón race had always been important: "There are some who say that Venezuela is a mixed-race country and that we're all one race of Venezuelans. But back then, when they oppressed the black, they didn't see it as, '*Coño,* he's from here, he's from our same country.' No, they didn't see it like that. They saw it as: 'He's black and we're gonna fuck him over 'cause he's black, he's not from our nation.'"

Given this militant language, why didn't gangsta rappers mobilize and make demands for racial equality? One possible reason was Venezuela's distinct history. The absence of race-based organizing in the postcolonial period meant that there were no models to draw on. In Cuba there were several experiments in racial mobilization—such as the Partido Independiente de Color, formed in 1908—but there were no corresponding organizations in Venezuela. This may have been because slavery ended in Venezuela much earlier than in other countries, such as Cuba and Brazil. While slaves in Cuba and Brazil developed coherent religious systems such as Santería and Candomblé, free blacks in urban areas of Venezuela began to absorb European culture and habits. Given the myth of a mixed-race, or *café con leche,* society during the postcolonial period, black identity and culture were even further submerged.

Another reason why gangsta rappers didn't organize was because they didn't have faith in the system to deliver racial equality. Unlike the Cuban rappers, who made demands on the state to live up to its promises of equality between the races, gangsta rappers in Caracas no longer trusted their corrupt politicians to lift them up from poverty and remedy racial discrimination. The solution was individual. They had to rely on their own forms of survival in the familiar terrain of the barrio. And they had to use their musical talents and entrepreneurial skills—honed through experiences in the drug trade and informal economy—to eventually bring themselves and their families out of poverty.

The members of Guerrilla Seca were not the urban revolutionary guerrillas of an earlier generation who would lay down their lives for justice. Rather, they were "straight-up guerrillas," as their name implied—they didn't have anything, they didn't buy into anything. There was no utopian vision that was worth fighting or dying for. As Requesón rapped in his song "La calle" (The street): "The world is shit and I'm addicted to this shit."

When I returned to Caracas in January 2005, life had returned to somewhat normal. In the August referendum people had turned out in a large show of support for Chávez, defeating the recall motion, just like they had defeated the coup a few years earlier. They were not about to let their president be taken from them so easily.

I had heard about new voices that were emerging in Venezuelan hip hop, and I was curious to investigate further. I could understand the appeal of gangsta rap for barrio youth, but it seemed that the culture of violence was reproducing itself, a vicious cycle from which there was no escape. How could music help to liberate young people from this chain of events rather than convince them that it was the only possibility? I had no doubt that the hypermasculine culture of *malandreo* was an incubator for forms of political consciousness and social criticism. But it seemed that challenging entrenched inequalities

© the author

Tupac mural, La Vega

was going to take a lot more. Was black *malandreo* the only kind of black militancy that existed among barrio youth? Or were there other revolutionary black currents that were developing in tandem with Chavismo?

My curiosity took me to La Vega, a large mountainous parish on the outskirts of the city. I took a bus from El Valle along the highway Cota 905, passing through a terrain of green hills with overgrown grass, and trees and plants with rich foliage. It terminated at the Centro Comercial, a large shopping center at the entrance to La Vega. But the expensive boutique stores and fancy pastry shops in the shopping center were mostly for the wealthy residents of neighboring El Paraíso. Cars and buses sounded their horns as they jostled to leave or enter the parish. Vendors lined the street with large glass cases of sticky buns and iced donuts, surrounded by a halo of bees.

I followed the road as it veered to the left, approaching barrio Carmen and the headquarters of the Afro-Venezuelan cultural group Grupo Autoctono de la Vega. Just beyond the small brick headquarters was a mural of Tupac Shakur, with a faint outline of Che Guevara's signature beret sketched in the background. Next to this was a mural of the Venezuelan flag, covered in graffiti tags. On a large piece of metal someone had painted a portrait of Malcolm X. Farther along this road was a small church and plaza, where fiestas of the black saints are celebrated.

In the plaza I met Black 7, Aja, and Ricardo Scó, members of the rap group Familia Negra (Black Family). They were young men in their early twenties who wore gym pants and basketball jerseys. Aja lived in an apartment block facing the plaza. We climbed the stairs to his apartment, a clean and well-kept space where his mother served us sodas. After drinking the refreshments we ascended to the open-air rooftop encircled by low walls patched together from flat bricks and concrete. It looked onto a sea of other similarly constructed rooftops and a few taller blue housing projects to the left.

Black 7, Aja, and Ricardo Scó grew up learning about the Afro-Venezuelan fiestas like San Juan and Cruz de Mayo that were celebrated in the small plaza of barrio Carmen. Before the 1980s these fiestas—which consisted of drumming festivals and parades—were held mainly in rural provinces with large ex-slave populations. But in the 1980s urban cultural organizations, like the Grupo Autoctono in barrio Carmen and other popular barrios, began to reclaim these cultural traditions as

© the author

Malcolm X portrait, La Vega

black culture and history. Local leaders like Williams Ochoa hoped to involve the young people of the barrio in the fiestas as a way of teaching them their cultural history and deterring them from a life of crime and violence. Black 7, Aja, and Ricardo Scó met through the Grupo Autoctono and carried its vision into their music.

"We belong to the real underground in Venezuela," Black 7 said. "What we do is different from what you hear in commercial hip hop."

"The rap groups you see on television here, they're all plastic," Aja added. "They wear baggy pants and jerseys, but it's all superexpensive gear because they're rich. Most of them are from the east of Caracas like DJ Trece. I'm not going to get up there and rap about being a *malandro*, because I don't live that in my reality. Me, for example, I'm a student and a worker. I can't turn into this rapper with a pistol and say that I'm the most *malandro* of all, that I live in a *cerro* and I was shot. I'd be inventing a fantasy. But that's what happens with a lot of rappers here.

"Society always wants to isolate us because we're against the system," Aja went on, "just like our martyrs, our ideological leaders like Martin Luther King, Malcolm X, Mandela, and Gandhi. We have suffered but we're not gonna suffer all our lives. We're going to open up paths. We're going to open the eyes of our fellow blacks. That's why we're called Familia Negra, because we try to raise the self-esteem of blacks who still today carry four hundred years of slavery in their blood.

"The constitution says that we're a multiethnic society, that here in Venezuela we don't have a defined race," Aja continued. "We're all *indios*, blacks, Arabs, Chinese, Portuguese, Spanish. It's a mixture, but unfortunately many Venezuelans continue with discrimination, and they don't realize that this is not a pure country. We look for our roots because one of the first martyrs of Venezuela who fought for independence was José Leonardo Chirino, a black who you don't find mentioned in our history books. By contrast, in the United States they have something called Black History, and this is how you learn to love your skin color and raise your self-esteem."

Aja's words resonated with me. In all my time in Venezuela, here, finally, was a perspective that I could fit into my understanding of the hip hop planet as a generation of young people across the globe who shared certain basic principles and ideals and wanted to use the music to advance a socially progressive agenda.

Black 7 found a portable boombox and played one of the tracks from their self-recorded CD. The song started with a simple background beat, then Aja rapping. I did a double take. He was rapping in English: "Yo, Black Family baby, Black 7 in the revolution, building my family / Fucking lexicon in the country jungles / Oh Latina, my color black, oh my nigga." Then he shifted into Spanish: "Representa mi gran poder, diversidad," and back to English for a series of phrases that were unintelligible. They sang on the chorus, peppered with American slang, "It's black emcee / Black family, once again yo / I'm a tall black powerhouse, ya know what I'm sayin.'"

They watched me expectantly. I hid my disappointment with a plastered smile. The most progressive politics didn't always produce good music.

All my travels seemed to confirm the idea that just as hip hop was very diverse in its origins, so it looked different as it spread across the globe. From the revolutionary rap in Cuba to Chicago's hard-core underground, Sydney's activist rap, and gangsta culture in Caracas, global hip hop was strongly shaped by local concerns. But did that mean that we were all so different that we couldn't come together or find common themes like race, marginality, or opposition to the mainstream around which we could unite? Venezuela seemed the perfect place to explore such a possibility, with a government that was willing to fund it. In January 2006 the Bolivarian government convoked a global hip hop summit in Caracas, complete with workshops, panels, and concerts.

"Suyee, we're in Caracas," Magia exclaimed over the phone. It had been years since I had seen my Cuban friends Magia and Alexey, who were invited to the summit. "We're scheduled to perform in the Rinconada at twelve-thirty today. Can you make it?"

"I'll be there!" I was excited to see them again and to be part of the summit that was bringing together hip hop artists from across Latin America and the globe for discussions of politics, art, culture, and how a global hip hop generation could be at the forefront of change. It fit nicely with my own quest.

Close to 12:30, I was approaching the Rinconada, a small auditorium behind the museum in the downtown Bellas Artes neighborhood of Caracas. Only a smattering of people were in the audience, and the stage did not seem to be set up for a show. I went to the front and inquired about the Cuban group Obsesión but was met with blank stares.

"No, *chica*, we're setting up for a folkloric event later in the afternoon," I was told by a plump woman with bright orange lipstick, who was preoccupied with sorting through a pile of fancy pink and blue costumes.

I had no phone number for reaching Magia and Alexey, and I had to be elsewhere later in the afternoon. An hour later I spotted Magia's signature brass-colored hair and Alexey beside her as they approached the Rinconada.

"Maaaaagia, Alexeeeeey!!!!" I shouted, and we collided into each other for long-awaited bear hugs.

"So it seems like you guys aren't performing here," I told them.

"That's news to us," Alexey shrugged.

"Ask them," Magia said to Alexey. She motioned to two white Cubans in shirts and pants standing behind us and talking into cell phones.

"Who are they?"

"Our chaperones," Magia confided in a whisper. "Sent by the Youth League, because apparently we need to be looked after here."

In a few minutes one of the chaperones came over and announced in a booming tone that the concert was to be held at another venue.

"I can't go," I apologized. "But I'll walk with you back to your van."

As we climbed the path out of the Rinconada, we were stopped by three Colombian rappers, who wanted an autograph from Alexey.

"You're our inspiration in Colombia," one exclaimed in awe.

The trio exchanged fist bumps and shoulder bang embraces with Alexey. "We're all the same, *los negros* in Cuba, Colombia, Venezuela, wherever," Alexey said, in the same warm tone he used whether speaking to his mother or a complete stranger. "We look the same, we hug the same, we even speak the same." I noticed that the Colombian crew didn't address or shake hands with Magia. She and I stood to one side as the greeting ritual took place.

The schedule of the hip hop summit was filled with panels on hip hop and the war in Iraq, social justice for the hip hop generation, hip hop and political prisoners, and international solidarities. It included plenary sessions to discuss where hip hop was headed as a movement. It sounded great—in theory. But somehow, each time I showed up, I found an empty auditorium with no participants or a completely different event. Venues were changed, directions were misunderstood, people were lost, and everybody kept missing each other.

Finally, at the end of the summit, there was to be a large televised concert in the plaza of the Panteón. I arrived with Johnny and Yajaira, and—no surprise—the large open square was empty. The stage had been erected, complete with a larger-than-life backdrop and high-tech speakers, while strobe lights scanned the vacant grounds. This was where my eleven-year journey had brought me—to an empty auditorium in Caracas, waiting for the finale of a global hip hop summit that would never happen. As we waited, I saw the parallels to global hip hop itself. Hip hop had galvanized the imagination of young people around the world, but it couldn't erase the differences between us or the difficulties of translating lives, cultures, and political visions. We were missing each other, literally and figuratively.

Global Rage: Over the Edge

In Caracas we were talking about Hip Hop for the People, planning an intervention of global hip hop against war and imperialism. Meanwhile, Paris was smoldering. On October 27, 2005, two French teens of Malian and Tunisian descent had fled to their death in an electricity substation in the Parisian *banlieue* of Clichy-sous-Bous after being harassed by police. Angry local residents in the poor communities across the city burned cars and defaced police stations and other public buildings. The French prime minister declared a state of emergency, establishing curfews and deploying national riot police. By November 17—just three weeks after the rioting had begun—there were about nine thousand torched vehicles, and police had arrested three thousand people in one hundred municipalities on the urban periphery.

The events in Paris bore similarity to the more contained but equally flammable situation in Redfern, Sydney, the previous year. On February 14, 2004, a young Aboriginal boy, Thomas "TJ" Hickey, rode his bike a few streets from his aunt's to his mother's place on the Block to collect twenty dollars. He was chased down by officers in a caged truck who were on the hunt for a suspect in a recent assault and robbery. Hickey was thrown from his bike, impaled on a metal fence, and subsequently died from his injuries. The next evening about one hundred angry youth staged a confrontation with police officers around the Redfern railway station. The street battle lasted for nine hours. For those familiar with the constant policing of Aboriginal communities, the revolt was no surprise. TJ's aunt, Virginia Hickey, told a reporter, "There are days when I would rather be dead than be an Aboriginal in Australia. I have experienced racism right through my life. There are shops and cafes we are not even allowed in. The police surveillance is 24/7. It is hard because all the kids know growing up is police, police, police."[1] Hickey's words echoed the rapper Ice Cube's comments after police were acquitted in the brutal beating of Rodney King, sparking the 1992 rebellion in Los Angeles: "It's been happening to us for years. It's just that we didn't have a camcorder every time it happened."[2]

In Clichy-sous-Bois, Redfern, and South Central LA, it was nothing as grand as an international caucus of hip hop activists and celebrities that had started the uprisings. It was something as routine as another act of police harassment, another young black person killed on the streets, that pushed people over the edge. It was here, at a street corner, or a railway station, that the fires of a generation in revolt were burning.

Rage was a defining feature of our times, and hip hop was a tool for expressing, catalyzing, and creatively transforming that rage into social criticism and musical innovation. Back in 1973, DJ Kool Herc created the sound system, Afrika Bambaataa launched the Zulu Nation, and Grandmaster Flash pioneered new techniques on the turntables. And around the world this movement catalyzed the passion, anger, and frustrations of young people who felt like they were living life on the edge of a precipice. Decades later "The Message" was still being echoed in the prescient raps of the French rap group 113: "There'd better not be a police blunder or the town will go up, the city's a time bomb." The question was not, why did the riots happen, but why didn't they happen sooner? "Why, why are we waiting to set the fire," rapped Suprême NTM from Seine-Saint-Denis.

Much had changed and much had happened in the eleven years since I started my journey. The world was now embroiled in the War on Terror, which heightened ethnic profiling in the metropolises. It meant the militarization of housing projects such as those in the *banlieues* of Paris; the harassment and detention of undocumented immigrants as suspected terrorists in American cities; and the creation of a Middle-Eastern Organised Crime squad in Sydney that targeted Middle-Eastern and Muslim communities. The myths of multiculturalism, social mobility, and racial democracy were being crushed under the weight of obvious disparities, and unforgiving cycles of poverty and everyday violence. Minorities were no longer to be assimilated and incorporated into the nation; their afros or baggy pants or veils were signs that they didn't belong and often made them targets of repression at the hands of the state.

My journey had brought me to various realizations. I had started out searching for the ways that hip hop culture could reignite protest politics on a global scale. I was hoping that the music could bring young people together across boundaries of nation, race, and ethnicity. And I did find moments of unity, mostly on the concert stage, as Cuban and American rappers celebrated their Pan-African identity; or a Nunga, Niuean, and Indian saw their common interest. But through the course of my travels I also saw the disjunctures between hip hop communities across the globe. KRS may have been called Kris in every 'hood around the world. But Kris was pronounced differently in the truncations of a Cuban accent, the laidback slang of a blackfulla, and a midwestern inflection. And 'hoods around the world were not identical, either. Global austerity and structural adjustment policies may have created similar cycles of poverty and violence among marginal communities. Yet a housing project in Alamar was not the same as one in Caracas; the South Side of Chicago was not the West Side of Sydney.

Race and racism—common tropes of hip hop culture—were not experienced the same way in different places. Hip hop emerged in American society, where people were used to talking about and identifying themselves racially—in both liberatory and discriminatory ways. But the culture spread to places where race was something to be ignored or denied as a threat to the social fabric. While hip hop's black militancy gave voice to experiences that were hard to otherwise articulate, it didn't always translate into local cultural understandings of race. At its best hip hop could create strength through recognizing the parallel lines of oppression that existed across cultures. At its worst it appeared as an American export that encouraged mindless imitation and imposed one narrative of race above others.

The racial politics of hip hop did not only appeal to black and African diasporic populations around the globe. It also spoke to Latino, Asian, Arabic, and, in some cases, even white hip hop fans. As George Lipsitz has argued, hip hop allowed these groups to become more themselves by identifying with something different.[3] Lebanese hip hoppers in Sydney or Asian and white rappers in Chicago were able to mark their difference from the dominant white culture by taking on African American style and culture. But creating a broader fellowship that would unite hip hoppers across racial lines required more than the rhetoric of international alliances and cultural borrowings. It depended on the existence of spaces of mutual interaction and experiences within the working-class areas and diasporas where collaborations could be realized.

Even the idea of a "brotherhood" that hip hoppers envisioned across cultures contained its own dynamics of gendered exclusion. When DJs and producers bonded at a DJ battle in a Chicago club, or Cuban and Colombian rappers exchanged fist bumps on a Caracas street corner, there was a sense of masculine camaraderie that left women looking on from the sidelines. Open mics and freestyle battles rarely had women participants. When women did take the mic, it was often with a different kind of presence, as Magia eloquently described it: "With their things to say, with their pain and happiness, with their knowledge, their softness, with the prejudice they suffer for being women, with their limitations, with their weakness and their strength." Many of the women artists in this book, from Magia herself to Ang 13 in Chicago and Waiata, Ebony, and Dr. Nogood in Sydney, brought this embodied awareness into their music and their lyrics. Female spaces within hip hop were to some extent separate. All-female concert series, such as the Sisterz of the Underground in the San Francisco Bay Area or the Proven Presence concert during the Havana rap festival, have been common ways to showcase women's performance.[4] But, as Magia said, separate concerts are also patronizing, as women are either "pitied or put on a pedestal."[5]

As I traveled, I learned that the global hip hop 'hood was more a fantasy than actuality. But at the same time hip hoppers were invoking the myth of a united hip hop fellowship to give more power to their localized movements. Cuban rappers drew on the idea of a black planet to boost their claims for recognition. Hip hoppers in Chicago and Sydney forged integrated spaces across racial and ethnic divisions as they built creative and political collaborations. And gangsta rappers in Caracas made strategic alliances across class boundaries that allowed them access to resources and enabled them to bring their stories to a wider audience. The broader connections of rappers gave them greater leverage to communicate and share their specific experiences.

I gradually came to understand the appeal of "The Message," which I had first heard as a teenager all those years ago. Expressing the everyday realities of "livin' on a see-saw" was what hip hop did best. It was why the music appealed so broadly across diverse cultures—not because everyone shared the same situation chronicled in the song but because it gave listeners an outline that they could color with their own experiences. Hip hop thrived around the world because it was a way for young people on the margins to tell their own stories—in all their hybridity, pain, and humor—in societies where there was no language or medium for these stories to be told. The strength of hip hop was not that it formed a grand global movement but rather in the myriad local forms of expression that it made possible. This was where the seeds of change were being sown. For some, like rappers in Havana and Sydney, the music spurred them on to political action. For others, like the underground artists in Chicago and Caracas, it became a tool for commerce. The sheer diversity of voices and politics that emerged across the hip hop globe made any attempts at a unitary protest culture impossible. And maybe even undesirable. For all its emancipatory promise, music couldn't substitute for politics.

As hip hoppers started to move across the globe, they developed new understandings of themselves and others that helped to break down some of the misconceptions that had plagued global hip hop. The diaspora was a base from which hip hoppers could create broader global networks and build multiracial solidarities. In some cases this was a result of hip hop artists' emigrating from their homeland, usually to Western countries like the US or Britain. Cuban rappers in particular began to emigrate after 2005. Following Julio Cardenas's departure for New York City in 2001, Ariel Fernández also left in 2005 for New York. The rap producer Pablo Herrera moved to Scotland. Miki Flow from Explosión Suprema went to Washington, D.C., Randy Acosta from Los Paisanos went to Caracas, and his rapping partner, Jesse Saldrigas, went to England. The encounter of Cuban artists with Latino artists in places like New York provided the ground for new collaborations. Julio Cardenas cowrote a play, *Representa!* with the Latino poet Paul Flores that dramatizes the dissonance they feel in each other's spaces. They are both minorities. But Flores is seen as a rich tourist when he visits Havana, while Cardenas has had privileges of education, health care, and social mobility under the Cuban revolution that are not easily available to marginalized Latinos in the US. The Latino-American-Cuban connection that Julio first imagined when he heard "Boricuas on Da Set" seemed to have a better chance of being realized when Cubans and Latinos could live in each other's spaces and acknowledge their differences.

In other cases hip hoppers in long-standing immigrant communities started to make contact with their ancestral homelands. Different ethnic and racial groups in Sydney had already come together in spaces such as the West Side and through the antiracism movement of the late 1990s. But in the new millennium some artists began to make global linkages with hip hop movements in their homelands. In 2002 Khaled Sabsabi made his first trip back to Lebanon in twenty-five years. He was interested in learning about traditional oral practices of improvised rhyming like *zajal*, chanting, and spoken word. He went back again a few years later to do studio training with young people across the country and in the Palestinian refugee camps. During the 2006 war between Israel and Hezbollah forces in the south of Lebanon, Khaled became involved with the Stop the War network. Following the war, through an installation project known as *Oversite,* he joined forces with Salah Saouli, a Lebanese artist based in Berlin, to look at how societies engage with traumatic experiences of war and how these devastating events affect the global diaspora. These two artists visited postwar Beirut and recorded the images, memories, and sounds that contributed to their artwork.

Through his travels between southwestern Sydney and Beirut, Khaled began to think about the dislocation of migration: What causes entire communities to be uprooted from their homelands, and how can they find meaning and direction outside their context? As he told Anna Bazzi Backhouse in an interview, "Living in South West Sydney is about being confronted with universal issues about migration, displacement, and the language of exiles—of diasporic communities searching for their sense of place and most importantly purpose. This is multiculturalism today—the ripping or legal theft of people from their lands, with the temptation and promise of a better life, away from political and economic unrest. Who is causing and who has caused this political and economic unrest in the first place?"[6]

The story of the global spread of hip hop is itself one of movement. A movement of ideas, a movement of commodities, a movement of people. If there is anything that marks this moment, it is as much the motion and mobility that bring us together as it is the boundaries and borders that divide us. Hip hop is a force defined by rupture and flow, and it remains to be seen whether global hip hoppers can reinvent themselves in the diaspora and build enduring links with their homelands.

As many of hip hop's pioneers, both in the US and across the globe, moved into other fields such as acting, filmmaking, theater, performance art, and community-based arts work, members of the new generation who were attracted to hip hop were mostly white. The interest from the music industry in exploiting the potential of local hip hop cultures led to a narrowing of the diversity of the culture. In Australia the vibrant early hip hop scene involving women, immigrants, and Aboriginals did not translate into commercial success for these groups. The Australian music industry promoted mostly white male rap groups as so-called Aussie rap. 1200 Techniques, the first Australian rap group to score a major label deal in ten years, was all white. The Hilltop Hoods, Reason, TZU, and The Herd—other groups to clinch record deals or have tracks on major compilations, get radio airplay, and inhabit the stages of Australian hip hop festivals—were also all-male, all-white groups, with what was deemed "crossover potential" by the record industry.

Poor black and working-class immigrant youth didn't have the resources to sustain their participation in hip hop over a long period of time. To make money as a rapper or b-boy requires some investment, which poor kids didn't have. Middle-class kids could more easily afford the samplers, turntables, spray paint, and records required for deejaying, producing, and graffiti. In places like Chicago, this included some middle-class black artists like Kanye West, whose English professor mother paid for studio time, bought his equipment, and tried to persuade him to finish his college degree despite his being pursued by record companies. As hip hop became mainstream, it also became more acceptable to white parents, who helped fund independent album releases, dance classes, or tours. Middle-class rappers also had more access to various kinds of cultural capital to support their work. In the summer of 2010 I received an email from a white middle-class rapper from Sydney who was applying for a Skills and Arts Development grant from the Australian Arts Council to pay for a trip to New York City. Doing hip hop was becoming less about a way of life and more about a professional career track.

Along with this, there was also a change in hip hop audiences. Fewer people participated in the elements of b-boying, rap, deejaying, and emceeing, and more people were attending rap concerts as consumers. Mike Treese experienced this for the first time when opening for a white rap group before a mostly white audience in Minneapolis in 2006: "Every show we always say, 'Where the hip hop people at? Make some noise! Where the b-boys at? Where the graffiti writers, DJs, and MCs at? Make some noise!' But all we heard were crickets. It was the first time I ever did a hip hop show where there weren't any hip hop people there. It was a dope responsive crowd who gave it up to us as the openers, but there was no breakers opening up a circle, no MCs cyphering."

One of the new paths to success for artists in an era of pre-packaged formats was reality TV. In 2006 Treese was approached to be a contestant on *The (White) Rapper Show* on VH1, wherein twelve rappers would live in a rundown South Bronx tenement and compete for the title of "great white emcee," along with a cash prize of $100,000. Treese turned it down. "You can't just take your art anywhere," he said, explaining his decision to me. "I don't want to get a deal because of a gimmicky TV show. I want it to be 'cause I'm good at it." Although being recognized for his skills was his goal, Treese started to question whether it would ever pay the bills: "Part of me knows that the dream was just to be dope, and that's it. So maybe my mind focused on that too much and I wasn't able to see the fortune and fame part. Or maybe the dream just didn't last long enough."

But even if the dream didn't last, the rage never diminished. The poor black youth who had created hip hop out of the tools of their everyday environment turned their creative energies toward other paths. Twenty-five years after b-boying had emerged in the South Bronx, a new form known as "krumping" took root on the streets of South Central LA. Emerging from the style of "clowning" developed by the party entertainer Tommy the Clown, krumping was a highly energetic dance with violent, frenetic, and fast thrusting movements. At its height of popularity in 2005, krumping counted about eighty crews throughout LA's ghetto neighborhoods. Krumpers were dubbed "the children of Rodney King," as their wildly flailing limbs echoed the movements of the brutal beating that defined their generation.

As my journey came to an end, I asked myself, what were the deeper personal reasons for my search for a global hip hop generation? It dawned on me that my search for a global movement was also a search for a perfect place, a search for belonging, a search for home. Growing up, I never felt that Australia was my home. I was always looked on as an outsider. I never felt that I belonged there—or anywhere. My travels showed me that there is no perfect place but that through community we can build a home. That is what hip hoppers were doing—they were building communities for themselves where they belonged.

As for me—for now I have settled in New York City, a place that is not perfect by any means but where an Indian-Australian-Portuguese gringa like me can be at home.

Notes

INTRODUCTION: THE MAKING OF A HIP HOP GLOBE

1. Derek Pardue, "Hip Hop as Pedagogy: A Look into 'Heaven' and 'Soul' in Sao Paulo, Brazil," *Anthropological Quarterly* 80: 3, 2007, 673–709.
2. Paul Gilroy, *The Black Atlantic: Modernity and Double Consciousness.* London: Verso, 1993.
3. George Lipsitz, *Dangerous Crossroads: Popular Music, Postmodernism, and the Poetics of Place.* New York: Verso, 1994, 27.
4. James Spady, H. Samy Alim, and Samir Meghelli, *The Global Cipha: Hip Hop Culture and Consciousness.* Philadelphia: Black History Museum Press, 2006.
5. Jeff Chang, *Can't Stop, Won't Stop: A History of the Hip-Hop Generation.* New York: Picador, 2005, 179.
6. Ibid.
7. Bakari Kitwana, *The Hip Hop Generation: Young Blacks and the Crisis in African-American Culture.* New York: Basic Civitas, 2002.
8. Chang, *Can't Stop,* 2.
9. Ibid., 183.
10. Ibid., 192.
11. Ibid., 228.
12. Jeff Chang, "It's a Hip-Hop World," *Foreign Policy* 163, 2007, 62.

13. Ian Condry, "A History of Japanese Hip-Hop: Street Dance, Club Scene, Pop Market," in Tony Mitchell, ed., *Global Noise: Rap and Hip-Hop Outside the USA*. Middletown, Conn.: Wesleyan University Press, 2001, 232.

14. Jesse Weaver Shipley, "Aesthetic of the Entrepreneur: Afro-Cosmopolitan Rap and Moral Circulation in Accra, Ghana," *Anthropological Quarterly* 82: 3, 2009, 644. Du Bois moved to Ghana toward the end of his life.

15. Sujatha Fernandes, *Cuba Represent! Cuban Arts, State Power, and the Making of New Revolutionary Cultures*. Durham, N.C.: Duke University Press, 2006.

16. Halifu Osumare, *The Africanist Aesthetic in Global Hip-Hop: Power Moves*. New York: Palgrave Macmillan, 2007, 85.

17. George Yúdice, *The Expediency of Culture: Uses of Culture in the Global Era*. Durham, N.C.: Duke University Press, 2003.

18. Eric K. Arnold, "From Azeem to Zion-I: The Evolution of Global Consciousness in Bay Area Hip Hop," in Dipannita Basu, Sidney Lemelle, and Robin Kelley, eds., *The Vinyl Ain't Final: Hip Hop and the Globalization of Black Popular Culture*. London: Pluto, 2006, 79.

19. André J. M. Prévos, "Two Decades of Rap in France: Emergence, Developments, Prospects," in Alain-Philippe Durand, ed., *Black, Blanc, Beur: Rap Music and Hip-Hop Culture in the Francophone World*. Toronto: Scarecrow, 2005, 9.

20. Dalton Higgins, *Hip Hop World*. Toronto: Groundwork Books, 2009, 34.

21. Ian Condry, *Hip-Hop Japan: Rap and the Paths of Cultural Globalization*. Durham, N.C.: Duke University Press, 2006.

22. Yvonne Bynoe, "Getting Real about Global Hip Hop," *Georgetown University Journal of International Affairs* 3: 1, 2002, 77–84.

23. Condry, *Hip-Hop Japan*, 33.

24. Sohail Daulatzai, "War at 33⅓: Hip Hop, the Language of the Unheard, and the Afro-Asian Atlantic," in Basu, Lemelle, and Kelley, *Vinyl Ain't Final*, 100–16.

25. Anthony Kwame Harrison, *Hip Hop Underground: The Integrity and Ethics of Racial Identification*. Philadelphia: Temple University Press, 2009.

26. S. Craig Watkins, *Hip Hop Matters: Politics, Pop Culture, and the Struggle for the Soul of a Movement*. Boston: Beacon, 2005, 138.

27. Chang, *Can't Stop*, 443.

28. Chang, "It's a Hip-Hop World," 64. Quite unexpectedly, even Cuban state radio features artists like Eminem while subjecting local acts to excessive scrutiny for obscenities before allocating them airtime.

29. Angela Steele, "Zai Beijing: A Cultural Study of Hip Hop," Undergraduate thesis, Stanford University, formerly posted at stanford.edu (accessed December 2008).

30. James McBride, "Hip Hop Planet," *National Geographic*, April 2007, 114.

31. Watkins, *Hip Hop Matters*, 96–7.

32. Wire MC, interview by Tony Mitchell and Nick Keys of *Local Noise*, May 31, 2006, Sydney, localnoise.net.au (accessed January 2008).

33. Nirit Ben-Ari, "From the South Bronx to Israel: Rap Music and the Israeli-Palestinian Conflict," PhD diss., City University of New York, 2010.

34. Watkins, *Hip Hop Matters*.

35. Harrison, *Hip Hop Underground*.

36. Prévos, "Two Decades," 15.

37. Fernandes, *Cuba Represent*, 91.

38. Chang, *Can't Stop*, 449.

39. Patrick Neate, *Where You're At: Notes from the Frontline of a Hip-Hop Planet*. New York: Riverhead Books, 2003, 117.

40. South African rapper Emile of Black Noise, interview by Cristina Verán, cited in Chang, *Can't Stop*, 451.

41. The rapper Common also goes by the name Common Sense.

42. Vanessa Díaz and Larissa Díaz, dirs., *Cuban HipHop: Desde el Principio*. Riverside, Calif., 2006.

43. Sunana Maira, "'We Ain't Missing': Palestinian Hip Hop: A

Transnational Youth Movement," *CR: The New Centennial Review* 8: 2, 2008, 161–92.

44. John Hutnyk, "The Nation Question: Fundamental and the Deathening Silence," in Basu, Lemelle, and Kelley, *Vinyl Ain't Final*, 125.

45. Justin Schell, "For Liberian-born Rapper Blade Brown Hip-Hop a Revolutionary Tool," *World HipHop Market*, July 3, 2008, worldhiphopmarket.com/blog/?p=1273 (accessed December 2008).

46. Ariel Fernández, Conference on "Hip Hop Cubano: A Showcase of Cuban Hip Hop, Culture, and Contemporary Art," Program in Africana Studies, Lehigh University, April 2008.

CHAPTER 1: MADE IN HAVANA CITY

1. Vanessa Díaz and Larissa Díaz, dirs., *Cuban HipHop: Desde el Principio*. Riverside, Calif., 2006.

2. Tricia Rose, *Black Noise: Rap Music and Black Culture in Contemporary America*. Hanover, N.H.: University Press of New England, 1994.

3. Imani Perry, *Prophets of the Hood: Politics and Poetics in Hip Hop*. Durham, N.C.: Duke University Press, 17.

4. In Cuba, *white* generally refers to a Cuban of European ancestry and ranges from those with blue eyes and fair skin to the more swarthy creoles. It is sometimes also used by light-skinned people of mixed-race background who wish to pass as white.

CHAPTER 2: DOWN AND UNDERGROUND IN CHI-TOWN

1. Anthony Kwame Harrison, *Hip Hop Underground: The Integrity and Ethics of Racial Identification*. Philadelphia: Temple University Press, 2009, 29.

2. William Upski Wimsatt, *Bomb the Suburbs*. New York: Soft Skull Press, 1994, 83.

3. Ibid., 107.

4. Ibid., 109.

5. Ibid.

6. The Maxwell Street Market on the Near West Side used to be the site of a bustling open-air market where street musicians performed blues and gospel, and street vendors sold a range of items, from car parts to household appliances. In 1994 the markets were shut down by the city in collusion with the University of Illinois at Chicago, who wanted to expand their campus into the area.

7. See Arnold R. Hirsch, *Making the Second Ghetto: Race and Housing in Chicago*, 1940–1960. Cambridge: Cambridge University Press, 1998.

8. S. Craig Watkins, *Hip Hop Matters: Politics, Pop Culture, and the Struggle for the Soul of a Movement*. Boston: Beacon, 2005, 91.

9. Kevin Beacham, "The Chicago Hip Hop Story," galapagos4.com, galapagos4.com/wp262/?page_id=89 (accessed December 17, 2010).

10. Wimsatt, *Bomb the Suburbs*, 125.

11. Wimsatt and Greg Kot, "Why Chicago Artists Have Been Outcasts of the Hip-hop World," *Chicago Tribune*, January 24, 1993.

12. Ibid.

13. Nona Gaye is the daughter of the soul singer Marvin Gaye.

14. Michael Schultz, dir., *Cooley High*, Chicago, Ill. 1975.

15. Harrison, *Hip Hop Underground*, 131.

16. DJ Rekha, "An Ear to the Streets and a Vibe in the Basement," in Ajay Nair and Murali Balaji, eds., *Desi Rap: Hip-Hop and South Asian America*. Lanham, Md.: Lexington, 2008, 164.

CHAPTER 3: BLACKFULLA BLACKFULLA

1. George Lipsitz, *Dangerous Crossroads: Popular Music, Postmodernism, and the Poetics of Place.* New York: Verso, 1994, 142.
2. Throughout this chapter, indigenous Australian group names will be used. *Koori* refers to indigenous people from what is today known as New South Wales and Victoria, and *Murri* refers to those from the region of modern-day Queensland. The *Wiradjuri* people are from the area of Central New South Wales.
3. Jock Collins, Greg Noble, Scott Poynting, and Paul Tabar, *Kebabs, Kids, Cops and Crime: Youth Ethnicity and Crime.* Sydney: Pluto, 2000, 109.
4. "Hip Hopera," *Life Matters*, ABC Radio National, October 1995.
5. The term *wog* was an ethnic slur originally applied to Greek and Italian immigrants in Australia but later used against those of Middle Eastern descent like Lebanese and Palestinians.
6. Yvonne Bynoe, "Getting Real about Global Hip Hop," *Georgetown University Journal of International Affairs* 3: 1, 2002, 77–84.
7. George Morgan, *Unsettled Places: Aboriginal People and Urbanization in New South Wales.* South Australia: Wakefield Press, 2006, 60.

CHAPTER 4: IN THE MOUTH OF THE WOLF

1. Kenneth Roberts, "Social Polarization and the Populist Resurgence in Venezuela," in Steve Ellner and Daniel Hellinger, eds., *Venezuelan Politics in the Chavez Era: Class, Polarization and Conflict.* Boulder, Colo.: Lynne Riener, 2003, 59–60.
2. Ana María Sanjuán, "Democracy, Citizenship, and Violence in Venezuela," in Susana Rotker, ed., *Citizens of Fear: Urban*

Violence in Latin America. New Brunswick, N.J.: Rutgers University Press, 2002, 87.

3. Yolanda Salas, "Morir para Vivir: La (In)Certidumbre del Espacio (In)Civilizado," in Daniel Mato, ed., *Estudios Latinoamericanos sobre Cultura y Transformaciones Sociales en Tiempos de Globalización II.* Buenos Aires: CLACSO, 2001, 244.

4. Eithne Quinn, *Nuthin' but a "G" Thang: The Culture and Commerce of Gangsta Rap.* New York: Columbia University Press, 2005, 22.

5. Imani Perry, *Prophets of the Hood: Politics and Poetics in Hip Hop.* Durham, N.C.: Duke University Press, 20.

6. Quinn, *Nuthin' but a "G" Thang,* 113.

7. Francisco Ferrándiz, "Malandros, María Lionza, and Masculinity in a Venezuelan Shantytown," in Matthew Gutman, ed., *Changing Men and Masculinities in Latin America.* Durham, N.C.: Duke University Press, 2003, 116.

8. Classic gangsta rap had its heyday from about 1988 to 1996 and involved artists predominantly from the West Coast and Southwest of the United States.

9. Robin Kelley, "Kickin' Reality, Kickin' Ballistics: Gangsta Rap and Postindustrial Los Angeles," in William Eric Perkins, ed. *Droppin' Science: Critical Essays on Rap and Hip Hop Culture*, Philadelphia: Temple University Press, 1996, 137.

EPILOGUE. GLOBAL RAGE: OVER THE EDGE

1. Susan Swarbrick, "A Boy, a Thief and a Martyr," *The Herald*, February 28, 2004.

2. Quoted in Robin Kelley, "Kickin' Reality, Kickin' Ballistics: Gangsta Rap and Postindustrial Los Angeles," in William Eric Perkins, ed. *Droppin' Science: Critical Essays on Rap and Hip Hop Culture*, Philadelphia: Temple University Press, 1996, 118.

3. George Lipsitz, *Dangerous Crossroads: Popular Music, Post-*

modernism, and the Poetics of Place. New York: Verso, 1994, 63.

4. Anthony Kwame Harrison, *Hip Hop Underground: The Integrity and Ethics of Racial Identification.* Philadelphia: Temple University Press, 2009, 166.

5. Margaux Joffe, "Reshaping the Revolution through Rhyme: A Literary Analysis of Cuban Hip-Hop in the 'Special Period.'" Working Paper no. 3, Andrew W. Mellon Undergraduate Paper Series in Latin American and Caribbean Studies, Duke University Center for Latin American and Caribbean Studies, Durham, N.C, 2005, 22.

6. "Ali or Eli," catalog for multimedia exhibition by Khaled Sabsabi, October 14–November 13, 2005. New South Wales, Australia: Casula Powerhouse Arts Centre and Campbelltown Arts Centre, 9.

Acknowledgments

I owe a big thank you to all of the hip hoppers in four cities who are the life and soul of this book. I'm glad that they trusted me that this would eventually become a book. Special thanks to Magia López, Alexey Rodríguez Mola, Pablo Herrera, Ariel Fernández, Randy Acosta, Julio Cardenas, Mike Treese, Jesse De La Pena, Waiata Telfer, Khaled Sabsabi, Munkimuk, Ebony Williams, and José Roberto Duque, among the many more who are mentioned in this book. I have tremendous respect and admiration for their work, and they contributed of themselves and their time to this project in ways for which I am incredibly grateful. I always envisioned this book as a coproduction, as explicitly collaborative as hip hop production and performance itself. In many respects these artists are also coauthors of this text.

There are several friends who helped facilitate my entry into these hip hop worlds and supported my visits around the globe. Lilia Cruz Marin and Norma Guillard Limonta were my companions and collaborators in Havana. Yajaira Hernandez and Johnny Moreno provided a place to stay and delicious *arepas* in Caracas. Anurima Bhargava introduced me to her hip hop people in Chicago. Antoinette Abboud and Maya Jupiter facilitated contacts and helped me reconnect with folks in Sydney. Bibi Serafim at Urban Theatre Projects in Sydney provided me with documents and information. Vanessa Díaz generously shared her materials from Cuba.

I am grateful for the insights of friends and colleagues who read drafts of the chapters and gave invaluable feedback. The idea originated with Miriam Angress, and even though it became something quite different from how it started out, I am indebted to her for the suggestion that I write the book. Jason Stanyek read several chapters at an early stage and gave me detailed feedback as to how I could turn it into the book that I wanted to write. Aoibheann Sweeney and the folks in the Mellon Humanities Seminar at the Center for the Humanities at the City University of New York Graduate Center gave me very useful feedback on my writing. Colin Robinson helped me make the transition from an academic to a nonfiction writer, and I am immensely grateful for all his advice over numerous lunches. Greg Ruggiero and Stephanie Griest gave me insights and suggestions about the trade publishing world. The project evolved significantly during my summer 2008 writing group with Joe Schloss, Lara Pellegrinelli, Kyra Gaunt, and Garnette Cadogan. I especially appreciate Joe's continuing feedback on the project after our writing group finished and Garnette's close reading and edits of my work. Kwame Harrison also read some chapters and offered very helpful comments.

I would like to acknowledge the indispensable work of my research assistant, Will Johnson. I am proud to use the photos of some terrific photographers—Oriana Eliçabe, Jason Florio, Sara Maneiro, Javier Machado, Sam Lazzaro, and Yoel Diaz Vazquez. I am grateful for a one-year Mellon fellowship provided by the Center for the Humanities at the CUNY Graduate Center to write the book. I also received funding from the Professional Staff Congress–City University of New York Research Foundation to support my writing. Thank you to the team at Verso for making the book happen, especially Sebastian Budgen.

My parents, Joe and Sylvie, as always deserve crucial thanks for all their help and support over the eleven years that I traveled and lived in cities across the globe. My sister, Deepa, and her partner, Matt Rogers, bore with me as I struggled with my writing, sharing their own insights and experiences of nonfiction writing. Thanks to my husband Mike Walsh and our children Aisha and Shaad for their loving support and even their interruptions, which gave me an excuse to play rather than work. This book is dedicated to Mike. Our animated discussions about hip hop over the many years of our companionship are reflected on every page of this book. He read several drafts and gave me his honest and unfiltered opinions. Without his challenging me to think and question myself, and helping me come to terms with my own relationship to hip hop, I would not have had the courage to publish this book.

All translations of Spanish lyrics are the author's. When lyrics have been used, the publisher and author have been careful to observe the rules of fair use. In any instance where the lyrics quoted exceed more than a few words, every attempt has been made to contact the copyright holder and obtain permission. The publisher apologizes for any oversight and will emend all future additions accordingly on being informed of the mistake. The author and Verso would like to express their gratitude to the following artists and publishers:

Untitled, by Ang 13, from the album *Ang 13*. Ang 13, 1999.

"Underground and Independent," by Capital D of All Natural, from the album *No Additives, No Preservatives*. All Natural, 1999.

"Boca de Lobo [Mouth of the Wolf]," by DJ Trece and El Nigga, from the album *Boca de Lobo*. Subterráneo Records.

Untitled, by Explosión Suprema. Unpublished.

"Black Malandreo," by Guerilla Seca, from the album *La Realidad Mas Real*. Subterráneo Records.

"Llegó el hampa," by Guerrilla Seca, from the album *La Realidad Mas Real*. Subterráneo Records.

"Tengo [I Have]," by Hermanos de Causa, from the album *Cuban Hip Hop All Stars, Vol. 1*. Papaya Records, 2001.

"Lágrimas Negras [Black Tears]," by Hermanos de Causa. Unpublished.

"Squash All Beef" by KRS-ONE, from the album *KRS-One*. Jive Records (Zomba Label Group), 1995.

"La llaman puta [They Call Her Whore]," by Magia Lopez, from the album *La fabriK: Obesión Doble Filo*. Self-published.

"How We Chill Pt. 2," by MC Juice and Rhymefest, from the album *Ritual of the …* Molemen Records, 2007.

Untitled, by Notorious Sistaz and Dr. Nogood. Unpublished.

"Run for the City," by Obesión. Unpublished.

"Everything That She Asked For," by Orishas, from the album *Orishas: a lo cubano*. EMI, 2000.

"El barco," Los Paisanos. Unpublished.

"Igual que tu [The Same as You]," from the album *Primera base: igual que tu*, by Primera Base. Caribe Production INC, 1996.

"Que Sera [What Will Be]," by Randy and El Huevo. Unpublished.

"Fuck the Brady Bunch," by Sujatha Fernandes and Waiata. Unpublished.

Untitled, by SWS (Munkimuk, Brothablack). Unpublished.

Untitled, by Treese of Mass Hysteria. Unpublished.

Untitled, by Two Indij. Unpublished.

"Historia nuestra," by Vagos y Maleantos, from the album *Papidandeando*. Subterráneo Records.

"Open Up Your Mind," by Ebony Williams. Unpublished.